Fei Xiaotong Studies
Volume I

《费孝通研究》第一集

Globalization of Chinese Social Sciences book series ①

中国社会科学全球化系列丛书 ①

Fei Xiaotong Studies

Volume I

《费孝通研究》第一集

Edited by

**Stephan Feuchtwang, Xiangqun Chang
and Daming Zhou**

With Assistant Editors Nick Prendergast and Costanza Pernigotti

GCP **Global Century Press**
全球世纪出版社

新世界出版社

Globalization of Chinese Social Sciences book series, Vol. 1

Fei Xiaotong Studies, Vol. I
Edited by Stephan Feuchtwang, Xiangqun Chang & Daming Zhou

This book first published jointly in 2015 by
Global Century Press
23 Austin Friars, London EC2N 2QP, UK
and
New World Press
24 Baiwanzhuang Road, Beijing 100037, China

ISBN 978-1-91033-404-1 (paperback, English); DOI https://doi.org/10.24103/GCSS1.en.pb.2015
ISBN 978-1-91033-405-8 (hardback, English); DOI https://doi.org/10.24103/GCSS1.en.hb.2015
ISBN 978-1-91033-406-5 (paperback, Chinese); DOI https://doi.org/10.24103/GCSS1.cn.pb.2015
ISBN 978-1-91033-407-2 (hardback, Chinese); DOI https://doi.org/10.24103/GCSS1.cn.hb.2015

British Library Cataloguing in Publication Data
A catalogue record for this book is available from the British Library

中国社会科学全球化系列丛书 第一卷

《费孝通研究》第一集
[英] 王斯福、[英] 常向群、周大鸣 主编

此书由以下两个出版社于2015年合作出版
全球世纪出版社
23 Austin Friars, London EC2N 2QP, UK
新世界出版社
中国北京市西城区百万庄大街24号

ISBN 978-1-91033-404-1 (平装·英文版); DOI https://doi.org/10.24103/GCSS1.en.pb.2015
ISBN 978-1-91033-405-8 (精装·英文版); DOI https://doi.org/10.24103/GCSS1.en.hb.2015
ISBN 978-1-91033-406-5 (平装·中文版); DOI https://doi.org/10.24103/GCSS1.cn.pb.2015
ISBN 978-1-91033-407-2 (精装·中文版); DOI https://doi.org/10.24103/GCSS1.cn.hb.2015

该书编入大英图书馆的公开数据中的图书馆编目

DOI https://doi.org/10.24103/en.namestyle

Global Century Press style rules for Chinese names

- Normally a Chinese surname (or family name) is composed of a single Chinese character (e.g. Zhao, Qian, Sun or Li), and occasionally two Chinese characters (e.g. Ouyang).

- In common usage Chinese names are written surname first (typically shorter), followed by first names (typically longer because they are composed of two Chinese characters, e.g. Wang Laowu, sometimes with '-' in the middle).

- In practice, overseas Chinese always put their surnames last in accordance with English name order, e.g. Laowu Wang. Some Chinese first names are composed of a single character, e.g. Zhang San, or ZHANG San, in some cases.

- In addition, some well-known names are based on conventional rules. Namely, they follow the order of Chinese names and do not capitalize surnames, such as: Fei Xiaotong, Zhang Yimeng.

- In our publications, if you see a surname in front of first names you can assume that person is mainland Chinese. All Chinese names are written in pinyin form, which is not italicized, as is the case for names of places, e.g. Beijing or Shanghai.

- There are exceptions, as individuals sometimes present their English names in their own way, which are acceptable.

全球世纪出版社中文名字英文显示体例

- 一般而言, 中文姓氏 (或家族姓氏) 由一个汉字构成 (例如: 赵、钱、孙、李), 有时由两个汉字组成 (例如: 欧阳)。

- 中文人名的写法, 在一般使用上, 先写姓氏 (一般较短的), 再来是名 (一般较长的) [因为它们由两个中文字组成, 例如: 王老五 (Wang Laowu), 有时候, 在中间加上分号 (-) 来连接人名的两个汉字。]

- 在实际运用上, 海外华人总是将他们姓放在最后, 以英文姓名顺序来书写, 例如: 老五王 (Laowu Wang)。有些中文人名由一个汉字组成, 例如: 张三 (Zhang San 或 ZHANG San)。

- 此外, 一些广为人知的名字的拼音根据约定俗成规则, 也是按照中文姓名顺序并且姓氏不用大写, 如: 费孝通 (Fei Xiaotong), 张艺谋 (Zhang Yimeng)。

- 在本社出版物中, 如果你看到姓放在名的前面, 你可以推测那个人是来自中国大陆。所有中文姓名由拼音形式呈现, 而不是以斜体字呈现, 地名也是如此, 例如: 北京或上海 (Beijing, Shanghai)。

- 名字的使用方式因人而异, 也有例外。

CONTENTS

DOI https://doi.org/10.24103/GCSS.en.0

General Preface to the Globalization of Chinese Social Sciences book series

Xiangqun Chang

The phrase 'globalization of Chinese social sciences' came out of a discussion with Professor Stephan Feuchtwang at the London School of Economics in 2010 about the title of a book commemorating the 100th anniversary of Professor Fei Xiaotong's birth. The first volume (in both English and Chinese) was published in 2014 by Global China Press alone and in 2015 jointly with New World Press. The dissemination of 'Chinese social sciences' covers a very wide range, in which the promotion of Fei Xiaotong's work is only the first step. We therefore decided to use 'globalization of Chinese social sciences' as the name of a book series in order to promote representative Chinese social scientific works. Here I shall briefly outline the key developments in 'Chinese social sciences' after 1949[1].

Institutions and resources

In China, the National Philosophy and Social Science Planning Group of the CPC Central Committee is the highest body in the Chinese social sciences. The group operates through the National Planning Office of Philosophy and Social Science. Its National Social Science Foundation is commissioned by the Department of Social Sciences of the Ministry of Education, the Research Bureau of the Chinese Academy of Social Sciences (CASS) and the Research Division of the Central Party School, to be in charge of universities, the institutions of CASS and the central State organs, respectively, with responsibility for the application of research projects, management of funds and evaluation of results. The National Philosophy and Social Science Planning Group also owns the National Social Sciences Database, which was established by CASS and developed by its Library in 2013. It is a national-level, open-information platform for Chinese social sciences. In 2015, the Chinese Social Sciences Year Book series (15 volumes to date) was published, representing the high standard of work in the field.

CASS consists of hundreds of research institutes, centres and related professional organizations, such as the Social Sciences in China Press (SSCP), Social Sciences Academic Press (SSAP), Chinese Social Sciences Net and its blogs and the journal Social Sciences in China and its site and blogs, the English version of which is now published by the Taylor and Francis Group. In 2015, the journal Social Sciences in China Review was founded. It aims 'to evaluate

---

[1] Before 1949 see: *Social Engineering and the Social Sciences in China*, 1919-1949, Yung-chen Chiang, (Cambridge University Press, 2006).

academic results based on national conditions, introduce a high standard of research results and create a system of academic discourse in contemporary China, comprehensively promoting Chinese philosophical and social scientific work in the world'. In recent years, the CASS Forum has also gained a strong reputation at home and abroad. In addition, there are a huge number of Academies of Social Sciences at province and municipality level. They also have their own publications on social sciences based on their work at the local level.

There are about 2,500 universities of different types in China. Some belong to the Bureau of Higher Education of the Ministry of Education, some to State ministries and commissions and others to provincial and municipal governments, and more one quarter are private universities[2]. In 2001, the Department of Social Sciences, Ministry of Education, built the humanities and social sciences services professional portal, the China Academic Humanities Information Network. It became the centre of information, online publications and the dissemination, management and public enquiry services for humanities and the social sciences. All the universities have different faculties and departments and research centres for different topics. Almost all have their own publishers, which publish academic journals and books. Social scientific work will be published in philosophy and social sciences edition. It is worth mentioning a few examples of universities' contributions to providing services or promoting Chinese social sciences at the national level.

In 1998, Nanjing University and the Hong Kong Polytechnic University developed a Chinese Social Sciences Citation Index and the academic series of the Chinese Humanities and Social Sciences Citation index. It led to the foundation of the Chinese Social Science Research Assessment Centre in 2000.

Tsinghua University and Tsinghua Tongfang Holding Group established China's National Knowledge Infrastructure (CNKI) in 1999. It was supported by the Education Ministry, Science and Technology Ministry, Propaganda Ministry and General Administration of Press and Publications, with self-developed cutting-edge Chinese digital library technologies and grid resources as a sharing platform. It built the most comprehensive system of Chinese academic knowledge resources – the China Integrated Knowledge Resources Database – covering journals, dissertations, newspapers, proceedings, year books, reference works, encyclopedias, patents, standards, S&T achievements and laws and regulations and some well-known foreign-language resources from Springer, Taylor & Francis and Wiley, forming a complete knowledge service network. The system is the core of the China knowledge resource base, encompassing a total of 101.9 million articles that include a large amount of social scientific work, some of which have been translated into English.

---

[2] 见：《2015年全国教育事业发展统计公报》，中国教育部(see: The 2015 National Education Statistics Bulletin, Ministry of education of China), 2016-07-06. http://www.moe.gov.cn/srcsite/A03/s180/moe_633/201607/t20160706_270976.html

Fudan University is a top-class locus for the internationalization of Chinese social sciences. It founded China's first national institute for advanced studies of social sciences (Fudan-IAS for Social Sciences). The founding Dean, Professor Deng Zhenglai, also founded the Chinese Social Science Quarterly in Hong Kong as early as 1992, which was re-established in 2008. In the same year, he founded China's first English-language journal on social sciences, the Fudan Journal of the Humanities and Social Sciences (FJHSS). Unfortunately, Deng passed away in 2013. His successor in Fudan-IAS, Sujian Guo, Professor of the Department of Political Science at San Francisco State University, USA, also became Editor of the FJHSS, which is now published by Springer.

Methodology

Some recent views need to be mentioned here. In 2011, Professor QIAO Xiaochun of the Institute of Population Research at Peking University gave a lecture entitled 'Chinese social science: how far away from science?' at a number of universities, including his own and Shanghai University of International Studies, China Youth University for Political Science, Huazhong University of Science and Technology and Zhongnan University of Economics and Law. He believed that Chinese social science occupies no position or status in world academia, and therefore enjoys no right of discourse. This is because methodologically Chinese social sciences have a strong speculative character, in contrast to the empirical studies on which general social sciences are based. However, in his 'Understanding the future' lecture in 2016, Professor Yu Xie of Princeton University and Peking University issued more balanced statements. On the one hand, he observed, scientific studies have three characteristics, namely objectivity, experience and repeatability. On the other hand, he put forward three principles, variability, social grouping and social context, which provide a methodological basis for social scientific research. Xie suggested that in today's China it is very important ever to carry out social scientific research on China scientifically since Chinese society has been changed all round significantly and still changing[3].

In 2014, XIONG Yihan, Associate Professor at Fudan University School of International Relations and Public Affairs, published an article entitled 'The internationalization of social science and native language scholarly writing in China'[4]. He criticized the phenomenon of 'academic nationalism' that wants to boycott internationalization, but also took issue with the 'colonial academic' who

---

[3]   谢宇：今天在中国做社会科学太重要了，也太幸运了，环球科学("未来科学"论坛演讲) [XIE YU, Today it is so important and so lucky to conduct social scientific research in China (a speech at the Future Forum, Beijing), *Scientific American*, 2016-07-26, http://oicwx.com/detail/1102356

[4]   熊易寒，中国社会科学的国际化与母语写作，《复旦学报(社会科学版)》，2014年第4期。[XIONG Yihan. The Internationalization of Social Science and Native Language Scholarly Writing in China, *Fudan Journal* (Social Sciences), No. 4, 2014.]

lacks local consciousness. He thought it very important that 'Chinese scholars should apply scientific research methods, actively participate in international academic dialogue and competition, invent dominant theoretical paradigms and set up research agendas with international colleagues. Even first-class Chinese writing with a global perspective is an integral part of the internationalization of social science in China.'

XIANG Biao, Professor of Social Anthropology at Oxford University, who graduated from the Department of Sociology, Peking University, in the mid-1990s, recently published an article on 'The ending of the "intellectual youth" era of Chinese social sciences'.[5]Scholars born before the 1960s, who received an incomplete education but had experience in rural China, have nearly all left their leadership or teaching posts. In contrast, post-1970s scholars, who received continuous formal education but without experience outside educational institutions, became the mainstream of academia. Xiang believes that the evolution of modern Chinese social science resembles the changes that have taken place between different generations of academic practice, knowledge acquisition and accumulation. Nevertheless, as Yefu Zheng, Emeritus Professor of Sociology at Peking University, pointed out, professors in the Department of Sociology at Peking University who were born before 1960 had still not retired; scholars' influence does not depend on their posts. Professor TIAN Song of Beijing Normal University also questioned whether the 'intellectual youth' era had ended. He maintained that the phenomenon of the post-1970s becoming mainstream is more of an academic management change[6].

Globalization of Chinese social sciences

The 'globalization of Chinese social sciences' is a live issue. The direction and outcomes of globalization of Chinese social scientific studies are neither Western nor Chinese, but add concepts, theories and methods derived from studying countries like China, which have a long history, huge population and complicated society, to the sum of human knowledge. This idea first appeared in 'A Chinese phase in social anthropology'[7], the Malinowski Memorial Lecture by Maurice Freedman given at the London School of Economics and Political Science in 1962. Two years later, Freedman made another speech on an occasion when area studies were being discussed, with the title 'What social science can do for

---

[5] 项飙, 中国社会科学"知青时代"的终结, 《文化纵横》, 2015年第12期。[XIANG Biao. The ending of 'Intellectual youth' era of Chinese social sciences, *Beijing Cultural Review*, No.12, 2015]

[4] 田松, 是代际替换, 还是制度变更? 《社会科学报》 2016年3月10日第8版 [Tian Song. Is generational change or institutional change? *Social Science Weekly*, Shanghai Academy of Social Sciences, 10th March 2016, p10]

[7] Maurice Freedman, A Chinese Phase in Social Anthropology, *The British Journal of Sociology*, Vol. 14, No. 1, 1963.

Chinese studies[8], in which he distinguished sinology from Chinese studies and emphasized the need to study China social-scientifically. Both Martin Albrow and Stephan Feuchtwang were research students, respectively in the Departments of Sociology and Anthropology at LSE, under the supervision of Maurice Freedman, and this affected their academic careers throughout their lives.

Martin Albrow helped many Chinese scholars to publish their articles in International Sociology in the 1980s when he was editor of the journal[9]. After 1990, he devoted himself to promoting the idea of globalization and became one of its international representatives. Nowadays, he helps promote Chinese social scientific work as part of the globalization of Chinese social sciences; at the same time, he attempts to insert the concept of transculturality into mainstream academia, as well as exploring the contributions of Chinese social sciences in the process of transculturalization. Details of this can be seen in my introductory paper launching the Journal of China in Comparative Perspective, entitled 'Transculturality and the globalization of Chinese social sciences: vocabulary, invention and exploration'[10].

Stephan Feuchtwang founded the China Research Unit at City University in 1973 when he worked there. It was the first organization dedicated to social scientific studies on China in the UK. Since 1998, when Feuchtwang was at the London School of Economics, he devoted himself to the creation of comparative studies of China. He appreciated Fei Xiaotong's comparative perspectives and theoretical conceptualization of the differential mode of association and organizational mode of association (Gary G. Hamilton's translation of 差序格局 and 团体格局[11]) and elaborated them with his own translation[12]. In 2013, after its gestation, birth and early years of growth of the China in Comparative Perspective Network (CCPN) at LSE, he supported changing its name from CCPN to CCPN Global, as CCPN completed the process of becoming independent from the LSE.

In addition to the above, some scholars are also dedicated to Chinese social sciences in the USA. For example, Professor Daniel Little, Chancellor at the

---

[8]   Maurice Freedman. What social science can do for Chinese studies, *The Journal of Asian Studies*, Vol. 23, No. 4, 1964.

[9]   Martin Albrow. A Chinese Episode in the Globalization of Sociology, *Journal of China in Comparative Perspective*, Vol.1 No.2, 2015. Its Chinese version see: 马丁·阿尔布劳, 社会学全球化过程中的中国片段,《中国比较研究》, 2015年第1卷第2期。

[10] Xiangqun Chang. Transculturality and the Globalization of Chinese Social Sciences: Vocabulary, Invention and Exploration, *Journal of China in Comparative Perspective*, Vol.1 No. 1, 2015. [常向群, 文化与中国社会全球化: 词汇的发明与发掘《中超文化国比较研究》, 2015年第1卷第2期]。

[11] Xiaotong Fei. *From the Soil: The Foundations of Chinese Society*, A translation of Fei Xiaotong's *Xiangtu Zhongguo*, by Gary Hamilton and WANG Zheng. University of California Press, 1992.

[12] Stephan Feuchtwang. Social egoism and individualism: surprises and questions from a Western anthropologist of China – Reading Fei Xiaotong's contrast between China and the West, *Journal of China in Comparative Perspective*, Vol.1 No. 1, 2015. Its Chinese version see: 王斯福, 社会自我主义与个体主义 —— 一位西方的汉学人类学家阅读费孝通"中西对比"观念的惊讶与问题,《中国比较研究》, 2015年第1卷第1期。

University of Michigan-Dearborn, presented a paper 'New developments in the Chinese social sciences' at a conference Mapping Difference: Structures and Categories of Knowledge Production, 19–20 May 2006, at Duke University. As early as 1989, he published Understanding Peasant China: Case Studies in the Philosophy of Social Science, which was translated into Chinese and published in 2009[13]. In 2010, Gary Hamilton, Professor of Sociology and International Studies at the University of Washington, presented a paper entitled 'What Western social scientists can learn from the writings of Fei Xiaotong'[14] at the international conference at LSE, Commemorating the 100th Anniversary of Professor Fei Xiaotong's Birth. Hamilton speaks highly of Chinese social sciences' methodological contribution to general social science methodology. A recent example was seen at the Young Scholars conference Social Sciences and China Studies, 20–21 May 2016, organized by the Fudan-UC Center on Contemporary China at the University of California, San Diego. These are joint efforts to promote Chinese social sciences from both Chinese and American scholars. All in all, a huge amount of work is being done all over the world in different disciplines studying China social-scientifically – too much to be mentioned here.

In the Preface of this book, Feuchtwang stated that Fei Xiaotong is probably the highest-ranking policy-influencing anthropologist ever, who profoundly influenced social policies in China's development[15]. In his Preface to *Peasant Life in China*, Malinowski noted that Dr Fei promised that after he returned to China he would work with Chinese colleagues to undertake the comprehensive reform of China's economic, social, cultural, political and belief systems[16]. Taking the opportunity of commemorating the 100th anniversary of Fei Xiaotong's birth to launch the initiatives of globalization of Chinese social sciences, is for promoting the results of comprehensive studies in China and Chinese society by Chinese and non-Chinese scholars into the human knowledge palace.

[13]   Daniel Little. *Understanding Peasant China: Case Studies in the Philosophy of Social Science.* (Yale University Press, 1989). Chinese version: 李丹《理解农民中国——社会科学哲学的案例研究》，江苏人民出版社2009年.

[14] Gary Hamilton. What Western social scientists can learn from the writings of Fei Xiaotong, *Journal of China in Comparative Perspective*, Vol.1 No. 1, 2015. Chinese version: 韩格理 (Gary G. Hamilton), 费孝通著作对西方社会科学家的启示, 《中国比较研究》, 2015年第1卷第1期。

[15] Stephan Feuchtwang. Preface, *Journal of China in Comparative Perspective*, Vol.1 No. 1, 2015

[16] Bronislaw Malinowski. Preface, in Hsiao-Tung Fei (Fei Xiaotong), *Peasant life in China*, London: Routledge, 1939.

DOI https://doi.org/10.24103/GCSS1.en.2015.1

Preface[1]

Stephan Feuchtwang

I remember Professor Fei with fondness; I think everybody who met him probably does. He smiled a lot, with a most benign look. But he was not at all complacent. Indeed, he was critical, curious and enquiring, as you can tell from his publications up to the very last. I would go further: he had such a strong sense of his own direction that it was difficult for me to know what he was making of what I said to him on the few occasions when we met.

Outside China and China studies he is not well known, and this is not surprising since he focused so resolutely on how his sociology and anthropology could help the Chinese people. He deserves to be well known for the fact that he is probably the most committed and eventually the highest-ranked policy-influencing anthropologist ever. But he certainly also thought of himself as a contributor to the social sciences, particularly sociology and anthropology, more generally. And he did not just study China. One of the points of this volume is to explore and expound his anthropology and sociology for a wider readership.

Each chapter, and the Appendix, contains what we consider to be contributions made by Fei's writings on China to a more general social science, either as a deliberately comparative concept or as a mode of analysis that can be applied elsewhere.

Fei Xiaotong's first contribution is his best-known and deliberately comparative conceptualization of the basis of Chinese social relations. It is a formulation invented by Fei, which is best left in Chinese: *chaxugeju*, two translations of which are expounded here – the differential mode of organization, and social egoism – compared and contrasted by Fei with secularized and Protestant Christian individualism. I would add, here, that *chaxugeju* is also comparable as a civilizational hierarchy in contrast to Hindu caste and sub-caste hierarchy, and the hierarchy of Euro-North-American industrial capitalist class and status, each with their own units of social mobility up and down the respective hierarchies, each encompassing from the top down in different ways. I hope to elaborate this comparison in a forthcoming book. In this book, apart from the various expositions of *chaxugeju*, there is also its extension and elaboration by Chang Xiangqun into a larger concept of interpersonal relations, *lishang-wanglai*, which takes into account a great many studies in China of 'face', the

---

[1] *Editor's note:* This Preface was written in August 2011. The author listed some of Fei Xiaotong's contributions based on the articles published here. After the event in memory of Fei Xiaotong's 100th anniversary at LSE 2010, the editors have received and collected many articles. Their views have not been included in this Preface.

art of connections, and the ethics of human relatedness, besides and beyond Fei's own. This elaboration is based on Dr Chang's own restudy of Fei's Jiangcun, namely the village of Kaixian'gong in Wujiang county, Jiangsu province, in the delta of the Great River, the Yangtze. But it is set, as Fei's original concept was, in readiness for comparison with other conceptions of interpersonal relations and their cultivation in other kinds of society. The discussions with Dr Chang in the Appendix bring out the possibilities of such comparison.

The second contribution is a continuation of the theme of comparison, but through a methodological imperative of self-reflection and self-exposition by anyone, native or not, embedded within a particular society but already partially disembedded by the task of studying it. Self-exposition refers especially to the untranslatability, or partial translatability, of the language of social reflection used by social actors in the society concerned. But exposition must persist in finding roundabout ways in another language of conveying what is not directly translatable. All the best ethnographies do this, without conceding to the obscurity of either a cultural relativism or a cultural chauvinism that reduces Chinese or any other culture to just itself. In some of his late publications, Fei turned this into a special kind of self-reflexivity. It is not the reflexivity of English-language anthropology celebrated in the widely read and followed chapters (except that by Talal Asad) edited by James Clifford and George E. Marcus in *Writing Culture* (Berkeley: University of California Press, 1986). In these chapters anthropologists seek to make explicit and to overcome the formerly implicit power relations between the anthropologists and their subjects of study. They seek to overcome these power relations by raising the statements and expositions of the subjects to a status equal to those of the anthropologists who bring them to the attention of a readership, while Asad points out the inherent and unavoidable power relation of writing in English. Fei's is a quite different reflexivity and has so far been confined to the Chinese language. It is a cultural reflection in which he uses the concepts derived from a culture to reflect upon itself, and crucially in addition to reflect on and with its 'heart' – the feelings as well as the reason and concepts that key words or phrases convey. One section of the Appendix expounds Fei's notion of 'heart'. Might there be a comparison and contrast here with a key text in English-language Cultural Studies, Raymond Williams' *Key Words* (Oxford University Press, 1984)? In any case, although confined to the study of China, Fei's example can be followed and varied by anthropologists seeking the culturally reflective terms of the societies and cultures they study and inhabit. And they would have to do this without insisting that only these terms are appropriate, because they want to be read in other languages and with other words and concepts, including those of the social sciences to which they contribute and into which they are finding roundabout ways to translate these culturally specific reflective words. Their very conceptualization depends on this effort of translation. Only by making this effort do they become applicable and open to comparison, though translation is merely a first step.

The second contribution is all about Fei's studies of villages in China. It would appear to be only about the study of China, no more and no less. But it does raise several more general methodological problems. Of what is a village study a so-called 'case'? And, if it is a 'case' of something claimed to be 'China', is it the appropriate unit of study?

One answer to the first question is to suggest that a village is an example of a 'community' and that Fei was following in the footsteps of the American Chicago School of urban sociology in pursuing 'community' studies, which are studies of localities within which most, but not all, relations in which the inhabitants engage are confined. Of course, urban studies since then have found just as often if not more often that the radiation of relationships from any one household goes far beyond their neighborhood and its radii do not coincide with those of neighboring households. They are especially differentiated by class and occupation. Similarly the relationships radiating, on the principles of *chaxugeju* and *lishang-wanglai*, from the households of a village are certainly not confined to the village but at the very least to a marriage area linking several villages, and those villages are linked in their economic activities with small towns. Fei was acutely aware of this and indeed he made small towns his basic unit of study after his classic village studies. This problem of the appropriate unit of study for qualitative fieldwork – within what range are most relations stemming from households confined in their coincidence, so that this unit is the best for intensive local studies – is common in a market economy and a state that defines the limits of local political relations. A good ethnography, precise in its descriptions, expounding well the local terms used for discussing social relations, is already a contribution to potentially comparable ethnographies and the economies and states in which they are set.

Then there is the question of how to generalize to the whole of that economy and state from selected case studies. Fei hoped to do this, first by village studies but then by small-town and regional studies, by comparing them and inducing from this comparison a typology of their differences, which were called, by him and by policy-makers, 'models' of different paths of development within the same political economy. Could this method be copied elsewhere, outside China? Perhaps. Could it ever become exhaustive, covering the full range of differences to be found in a country at one time? I doubt it.

Finally, there is the question of what is a study a 'case'? Were Fei's studies cases of economic development or more? They can as well be read as case studies of gender relations, or of kinship relations, to be compared not only within China, as in Chapter 4, but with other such case studies from other contexts altogether, of development, of gender relations and of kinship relations.

The fouth contribution continues with a discussion of these questions: how and for what were Fei's studies carried out, and how can they be extended to other studies in China up to the present day? But in this chapter we come to Fei from the opposite direction, in fact from two directions. One is from outside China to his concepts. The very question of whether Fei's work, in his own estimation, should be a contribution to the 'luxury' of anthropological theorizing is raised in relation to the work of English anthropologists. Concepts from general sociology, chiefly that of urban Euro-North-America, are applied to his concepts of *chaxugeju* and economic enterprise. Readers will have to settle for themselves whether these outside concepts have to be changed in their application to Fei's Chinese concepts and studies. What further steps must we take in accepting Fei's works into anthropology, or into the sociology of social capital, or into management studies?

The other direction is from his work on other peoples in China than the Han majority to the question of 'China'. What is 'China' as bounded by its present borders, including the large border regions that Fei helped to define? How different are these border regions from the other regions of China? More currently, less historically, how are their separate paths of development, or modernizations in the plural, to be nurtured and acknowledged even as their differences grow while their sharing a state and an economy brings them together? Several potential comparisons suggest themselves, for instance with the Russian Federation of States or with India's adivarsi (tribal peoples), though none have been carried out yet.

The fifth contribution based on an article we come at last to some country-to-country comparisons, though they must be suggestive of the far greater potential for comparison. Comparison of kinship systems, based on Fei's Kaixian'gong, and of border regions based on his Chinese border region studies, are the most anthropological. Comparison of the construction of garden cities as communities with Fei's small-town studies and policies is more sociological and has more to do with planning. And two further reviews of the relationship of Fei's anthropology to general and comparative studies extend the discussion relating to the second and the fourth contributions.

Finally, the six contribution is about Fei's life and work, indeed to his life as a work of Chinese political history. In his later years and since he died China has become a world power of which the rest of the world has necessarily taken notice, not least the social scientists of the English writing world. Coming from several disciplines and not specializing in the study of China, some of them seek and find in Fei's works at least two things. One is a set of clues to the workings of Chinese society. The other is his example and the way in which the study of China can be an example of world anthropology or global sociology. Again the potential is clear, but its realization is yet to be accomplished. And that is the message of every part of this book. The potential for comparison, contrast, and contribution to general social sciences has, we hope, been made clear. Its realization is to be accomplished by further work.

DOI https://doi.org/10.24103/GCSS1.en.2015.2

Transculturality and the Globalization of Chinese Social Sciences
Vocabulary, Invention and Exploration[1]

Xiangqun Chang

This paper falls into five parts: raise the matter of transculturality, the importance of transculturality and invented Chinese social science vocabularies in understanding China and the world; the significance of inventing and developing Chinese social science vocabularies; Fei Xiaotong's contributions to Chinese social science vocabularies and the globalization of knowledge; and comprehensive understanding in China's social sciences and transcultural experiences in the process of the globalization of knowledge. In sum, we will consider, on the one hand, 'the creation and development of the vocabularies of the Chinese social sciences' as a part of global knowledge construction; and, on the other hand, the structure of Chinese society and its operational mechanism in a global context.

Transculturality matters

In 2014, CCPN Global and YES Global successfully organized the First Global China Dialogue in London, with the theme of 'the experience of China's modernization from a comparative perspective'. Arising out of this was the stark realization that today's world faces numerous risks and challenges on the road to peace and development. The international system and order are constantly changing, as is the balance of power. In such an era of great transformation, all countries, whether developing or developed, are having to adapt to an ever-shifting international and social environment, while the process of modernization in some countries has been interrupted or has spilled out to create global turmoil.

At the same time, rapid developments in technology and society have had a profound impact on patterns of thinking, behaviour and interaction and on the moral principles of different countries and groups. They have also constantly challenged established ideas of good governance, including the functions of government in the globalization era and the pros and cons of the participation of non-government organizations. The changes and challenges are myriad: digital technology, mobile

---

[1] This is a so-called 'by way of introduction' for the launch issue of the *Journal of China in Comparative Perspective*. (vol.1 (1), 2015). It has been slightly modified here because it would be helpful for understanding the theme of this volume, though some contents do not directly relate to Fei Xiaotong's work. Many thanks to scholars and colleagues, including Professors Stephan Feuchtwang, Martin Albrow and Sam Whimster, Dr Dongning Feng and Mr Xiaowei Xiang, for their valuable comments and suggestions.

communications and the popularization of the internet, the coexistence of cultural homogenization and diversity, ethnic and religious conflicts, the collision between giant multinational corporations and national sovereignty, changes in social norms as a result of scientific innovations, the decisive influence of regional economies on national economic development, the constraints of climate change and the discovery and adoption of new energy sources. Transculturality has become part of people's daily life. It is different from cross-culture, inter-culture and multi-culture.

Confronted with such challenges, national leaders devise development strategies that reflect both the status quo and their long-term goals. Business leaders and entrepreneurs have also invested substantial resources in studying the impact of the changing international economy and financial order on the development of enterprises. Experts and scholars have focused on cultural factors that have quietly exerted great influence, and explored how culture and ideology enhance global and social governance. Such efforts and initiatives are moves in the same direction: towards reaching an in-depth understanding of the knowledge systems of the human community and the development of a 'global cultural sphere' beyond any single culture, state or nationality, under the condition of global governance. Thus, the theme of the development and governance of China, Europe and the world has gradually become one of the key research interests of scholars worldwide.

There are already many work and activities on transculturality in the past two decades. For example, uccioletta 2001/02, Flüchter & Schöttli 2015, Lewis 2002, Schachtner 2015, Slimbach 2005, Welsch 1999. In addition, there are some organizations that either publish specialized journals or organize related events: the Institute for Transtextual and Transcultural Studies publishes *Transtext(e)s–Transcultures: A Journal of Global Cultural Studies*; the Transcultura International Institute holds the China–EU Intercultural Forum jointly with the Chinese Academy of Social Sciences (CASS); at Columbia University there is a Department of International and Transcultural Studies; and an International and Transcultural Communication Programme exists at Universität Salzburg. Some universities have related research centres, e.g. Centre for Transnational and Transcultural Research, University of Wolverhampton; Research Centre for Transcultural Studies in Health, Middlesex University; International Center for Transcultural Education, University of Maryland; Heidelberg Centre for Transcultural Studies. In China, Peking University founded the Center for Cross-cultural Studies and has published the journal *Dialogue Transcultural* (in Chinese) since 1998. It collaborates with the Institute of Comparative Literature and Comparative Culture, Nanjing University; the Institute of Cross-cultural Studies, Chinese Culture Academy; the Institute of Chinese Folk Culture, Beijing Normal University; and the Transcultura International Institute; and is supported by the Mayer Foundation for Human Progress. A significant development is the founding of the Beijing Forum – The Harmony of Civilizations and Prosperity for All, founded jointly by Peking University, Beijing Municipal Education Commission and the Korea Foundation in 2004, which will hold its 12th Forum on 6–8 November 2015 with the theme of 'different roads and shared responsibility'.

Against this background, CCPN Global, JCCP and *Global China Dialogue* series[2] will engage broadly and work cooperatively, based on the above existing studies and activities to promote an all-round concept of transculturality, to push it from a marginal position towards the centre of mainstream discourse among academics, intellectuals and thinkers worldwide. This will provide both an in-depth and comprehensive understanding of the history of our era and accurate forecasts of the trends in development of human society.

Transculturality, the importance of invented Chinese social science vocabularies in understanding China and the world[3]

The first article for JCCP's launch issue was chosen for its ingenuity. In 'Universal dream, national dreams and symbiotic dream: reflections on transcultural generativity in China–Europe encounters', Shuo Yu reinterprets a very complicated historical case, demonstrating not only an ability to carry out a study on China in comparative perspective but also to cross disciplines from social sciences to linguistics, showing how translation in social–cultural contexts can make a huge impact on the direction of history.

One of the major contributions of this article is that it introduces a self-made new concept of 'transcultural generativity'. The article creatively applies the 'transcultural approach or perspective' to a large social and historical field, through analysis of the encounters between Western missionaries and the Imperial Court of the Qing dynasty. In doing so, it finds evidence for 'transcultural generativity' by demonstrating how both parties work together creatively, in direct or indirect interactions, and by exploring the mechanism of such encounters. As the author shows, the results of these encounters are neither Hannization nor Westernization, but a dynamic 'permanent transition' from a marginal position to create a third

---

[2] The Second GCD will be held on 23-24 November 2015 at the British Academy. 2015 is the Year of UK–China Cultural Exchange. This event will demonstrate transcultural practice by collaborative working between academia and governments in China and the UK, with support from international organizations and academic NGOs, and also showcase Chinese academia's participation in regional and global governance. It will discuss all facets of new global governance, encompassing national governments, international organizations, multinational companies, NGOs and citizens, as well as seeking new rules of 'civilized dialogue', encouraging both sides to listen to the other, understand cultural differences, respect local customs, accept different perspectives and acknowledge the common destiny of humanity, with a view to building a harmonious, symbiosis-based global community

[3] Here 'China and the world' is a short way of saying 'China and the other countries and regions of the world'.

category of shared knowledge and values. This hybridization inspired the new banner image on the CCPN Global website[4].

Yu's article links the past to the present with three categories of dream: universal dream, national dream and symbiotic dream. As the author points out, 'The 21st century has to be a collaborative century, the global good and evil forces are composed of diverse coalitions'. 'Transcultural generativity' could help us to understand how global society is shaped and reshaped. Further, how the concept of 'transcultural generativity' is worked out can be understood from a set of vocabularies, such as liminal space, permanent transition, cultural agency of the in-between, China–Europe encounters and a symbiotic dream of the Earth. Although these vocabularies were derived from studies of interactions and relationships between China and the West over the past centuries, they are new for both Chinese and non-Chinese readers. It is also a question for academic research whether or not they have a place in the list of general social science vocabularies.

Moreover, the key concept of 'transcultural generativity' highlights JCCP's ethos of creativity and echoes the theme of this issue, which is the creation and development of the vocabularies of the Chinese social sciences. The author's invention of large numbers of transcultural anthropological terms is a concrete exercise bringing elements of Chinese culture to a wide audience, which accords with CCPN Global's academic mission. Finally, CCPN Global's social mission, as a bridge between China and the rest of world, the Chinese and the non-Chinese, is destined to inherit the spiritual legacy of the 500-year history of China–Europe encounters. We therefore see this article as symbolic, demonstrating the actual character of JCCP and CCPN Global, the virtual community of symbiotic humanity. We hope to enhance people's sense of community, the power of thinking with cultural diversity and complexity and the revival of a symbiotic ethical spirit[5].

The significance of inventing and developing
Chinese social science vocabularies

In choosing the theme of this launch issue of JCCP, the aim was to build a bridge between Chinese and Western social scientists who are dedicated to making contributions to human knowledge. There are two viewpoints in Western social science: one is that the level of Chinese social science is generally low; the other is an expectation of learning from relevant research by Chinese scholars. The first article in this issue of JCCP was written by a historical anthropologist who trained in both China and France and now works in Hong Kong. This article clarifies a complex transcultural and historical phenomenon through description and analysis

---

[4] The new banner image on CCPN Global's homepage (www.ccpn-global.org) is adapted from a painting entitled *Fourmillements* ('Swarming', 132 x 162 cm, acrylic on canvas, 1985), by François Bossière.

[5] Unfortunately the author suffered an accident and was consequently unable to revise the article, which caused a delay in publishing this issue.

with rich vocabulary and terminology. It demonstrates a Chinese scholar's global vision and humanity. The second is a study by an American social anthropologist on the theory and method, and especially the vocabulary, employed by Chinese social scientist Fei Xiaotong in his research. The next article is a Swedish sinologist and lawyer's commentary on the application of Fei Xiaotong's methodological viewpoint. The articles that follow were written by scholars from the USA, the UK and Germany. They demonstrate, on the one hand, Chinese scholars' efforts to produce innovative ideas on a normalized social scientific basis; and, on the other hand, non-Chinese scholars' attempts to re-evaluate and properly understand, through in-depth studies, Chinese scholars' work. Both Chinese and non-Chinese contributors are engaged in self-reflection in doing research on China, while at the same time going beyond their own cultural limitations.

In Chinese social science circles there are also two prevalent perspectives: the first is that Chinese study by foreign scholars yields only ineffective solutions for practical problems; the second is that the Chinese should 'break out from Western academic hegemony'. This so-called 'Western academic hegemony' includes aspects of language and discourse. It can be seen in the publishing of articles in English, in the practice of writing in accordance with Western social science norms and styles, in authors being accepted by the Western academic system, and in works being understood according to Western ideology. To Chinese scholars, these requirements are seen as an 'academic hegemony', a viewpoint shared even by acknowledged great scholars such as Fei Xiaotong, only a few of whose works have been published in English because his extensive writings have not yet been translated. And even if these works were translated into English, the English version might not always accurately express the essence of his academic thought. Thus it has little power in the discourse of the field studied. In the following, we will see detailed related views.

First, there is a basic problem with publishing articles in English. The International Sociological Association recognized this when it established its journal *International Sociology* in 1986, giving special consideration to papers submitted by those whose first language was not English, reviewing them in their first language by in-culture specialists and helping them with translation. With these aims, Dai Kejing of the Chinese Academy of Social Sciences and specialists from other language communities were appointed as Associate Editors (Albrow 1987). The editorial input was correspondingly heavy and expensive, but fully justified by the editor in an analysis after four years showing acceptance during that time of a higher proportion of submissions from non-first world countries than from the first world (Albrow 1991: 111).

Having foreign editors for English-language journals is made all the more necessary in view of the 'warning' by the British Academy, mentioned by Steven Harrell in his article, about 'a decline in modern language learning' (2009) in the UK. A report entitled 'Language Matters' 'discussed concerns that the future of the UK's world-class research base might be threatened by the decline in modern language learning and calls for a series of measures by universities and government bodies to address this danger.' This was one justification for the construction and expansion of CCPN's bilingual website when it was at the LSE. 'Language Matters More and More' was published by the British Academy in 2011. The question of how to 'build the capacity of the UK's knowledge economy to meet national and international challenges' is relevant here, not because of the language learning, but for gaining a better understanding of the meanings behind English and Chinese languages within a social, cultural and economic context. The decision by CCPN to turn JCCP into a dual-language periodical can be seen as a positive response to this warning. The title of the British Academy's report in 2013 is 'Languages: The State of the Nation'. In its preface, Professor Nigel Vincent, Vice President of the British Academy, points out that 'languages are vital for the health and well-being of the education and research base, for UK competitiveness, and for individuals and society at large' (p. 8). JCCP has set up a section called Chinese for Social Science, which aims to help the world's increasing numbers of Chinese language learners who are interested in social science topics. By reading our articles, they can improve their language abilities in meaning, context, discourse, translation skills and so on, and gain a deeper understanding of the related research article.

In the Preface, Professor Stephan Feuchtwang mentions two kinds of 'translation problems': one is the everyday translation from one language into another (this step is relatively easy); the other is the translation of culturally specific reflective words, which is a knowledge creation process requiring the participation of both social scientists and linguists.

Gao Bingzhong, Professor of Anthropology at Peking University, who did his postdoctoral research under Fei Xiaotong's supervision, takes a different path. In 2002, he launched the 'overseas ethnography' programme, and led students to engage in anthropological fieldwork in a dozen countries around the world. They 'rewrite anthropology in Chinese' and have published more than ten ethnographies in Chinese. It is hoped that Chinese social science research will move from the empirical study of Chinese society to 'world society' (Fei Xiaotong proposed the concept in Chinese in the 1940s). This work would be more meaningful if the publications could be translated into English and thus compared with other English works. By comparing the similarities and differences between English and Chinese work on the same topics in the same region, it may be possible to gain a more comprehensive understanding.

Second, there is the issue of the writing of articles that conform to Western social science's norms and styles. The academic norms and standards are very broad, from the methodology and the specific research method to the style and organization of the writing. In the next issue we will publish an article by Gary Hamilton. He points out that 'writing in a foreign language about a foreign place has not stopped Foucault or Habermas or Bourdieu from developing wide readerships in the US', so, why cannot this be the case for Fei Xiaotong's works? Hamilton thinks this is because of Fei Xiaotong's implicit writing style and his personal character. In fact, this kind of implicit (hanxu) prose style can represent a writing style of Chinese 'literati scholars' (Chang 2010 [based on PhD dissertation 2004]; Zhai 2006). Hamilton also pointed out that, from the Western perspective, in view of the limitations of many Chinese scholars when it comes to understanding Western theory, Chinese scholars also cannot totally understand the theoretical depth of Fei's book Xiangtu Zhongguo. So, he sets the study of Fei Xiaotong in the framework of a comparative study of East and West.

In contrast, methodologically, Feuchtwang mentions in his Preface that anthropologists are seeking to make explicit and to overcome the formerly implicit power relations between anthropologists and their subjects of study. He thinks that an outstanding ethnography can, in a roundabout way, use another language to convey meaning that cannot be translated directly. I believe two good examples of this are Fei Xiaotong's *Peasant Life in China* (1938), a descriptive ethnography, and Yan Yunxiang's *The Flow of Gifts* (1996), which also contains, compared with Fei's work, a more in-depth study of the theoretical and methodological aspects of ethnography. However, outstanding works on Chinese society that are both written in English and follow social science norms are very rare in the world. If Western social scientists rely solely on these few research results to develop their theories, then world-class standards will indeed decline, as the British Academy warns.

Interestingly, in his own Preface to the Chinese version of *The Flow of Gifts* (1999), Yan apologizes to his Chinese readers that he does not include reviews of relevant studies by Chinese scholars. This suggests various questions. Is the best work by Western standards the best by Chinese standards? How can we understand the power relationship between researchers and subjects when the different methodological implications of 'implicit' and 'explicit' have been exercised in Chinese and in Western ways while studying global society, including both Chinese and non-Chinese societies? Do we have standards to judge which way is better? Who sets these standards?

Third, there is the problem of authors being accepted by the Western academic system. For centuries, ancient Chinese philosophers such as Confucius, Lao Tzu, Chuang-tzu and Sun-tzu have been introduced to Western countries by sinologists and included in textbooks. Chinese writers such as Gao Xingjian and Mo Yan were even awarded the Nobel Prize for Literature. However, how many contemporary Chinese social scientists have ever been recognized in the West? For example, according to 'A Report on Academic Influence of the Research Achievements in the Humanities and Social Sciences in China (2000–2004)' (Su 2007), Deng Zhenglai is ranked in the top 50 in six different disciplines, placed first in law, second in political science and fifth in sociology. But who in the Western academic world knows which of Deng Zhenglai's academic ideas have been widely cited in Chinese academic circles? Deng passed away early in 2014 at the age of 56. Would it be possible for Deng, as a 'self-employed academic scholar' (*xueshu getihu*) for 18 years in China, ever to be of interest to Western scholars?

Indeed, although it appears that Chinese scholars' academic thought is rarely recognized by Western social sciences, this would not be altogether impossible. With the encouragement and support of Professor Martin Albrow, the former President of the British Sociological Association, CCPN is compiling two series of books: one is *Social Science: Key Concepts from a Chinese Perspective* and another is *Chinese Thoughts for a New World Order*. We hope to start from a concept, a point of view, with cooperation between the authors and the translators, and then gradually to add Chinese social scientific and academic thinking to the repository of human knowledge. In addition to these, Global China Press is planning four other series of books: *Chinese for Social Sciences*, *Chinese Discourse*, *Understanding China and the World*, and *Examining China and the World with 'Three Eyes'*. This last book series will consist of popular social scientific books that use storytelling to promote mutual understanding between China and the world, Chinese people and non-Chinese.

Finally, we consider the topic of being understood by Western ideology. In the 1980s, there was a saying in Chinese academic circles: 'Masters stand outside institutions' (*tizhi wai dashi*). Deng Zhenglai, mentioned above, can be seen as one such case, although he was made Founding Dean of the Institute of Advanced Studies in Social Science, Fudan University, a few years before the end of his life. Karl Marx was in fact named in the 1980s by Chinese scholars as one of the 'masters outside institutions'. Although he was not employed by any university, he created more abundant knowledge products than most university professors and these have entered the textbooks in all mainstream universities. This may be because Marx's world view, methodology and academic norms are now part of the Western academic knowledge system, the innate factor that allows the possibility for his writing to be accepted in mainstream academic circles.

However, for Chinese social scientists, in addition to the language, the academic standard and its system, the problems of ideology and related methods also play an important role in the process by which Chinese academic theory and method gain acceptance into Western academic circles. For example, in his Preface, Feuchtwang mentions two people: one is Asad, who points out the inherent and inevitable power relations in English writing; the other is Fei Xiaotong, the reflective characteristics of whose writing have not become well known in the English academic world. Feuchtwang states that 'it is a cultural reflection in which he uses the concepts derived from a culture to reflect upon itself, and crucially in addition to reflect on and with its "heart" – the feelings as well as the reason and concepts that key words or phrases convey'. He also suggests that this can be compared with related content in the book of *Keywords* by Raymond Williams (1984).

In order to explore these issues, JCCP will publish related articles comparing Andrew Kipnis's 'nonrepresentational ethics' (1997) and *Human Mind* (the Chinese title can be translated into English as 'Human Life and Human Heart') by the Chinese master Liang Shuming (1948). This brings us to the question of how we should use complex vocabulary independently of the socio-cultural context. In the last article of the current issue, Harro von Senger discusses how to overcome the earthbound 'encoded eye' problem (Foucault 2008). He quotes Foucault's point of view that Westerners should be conscious of their 'encoded eye', which is governed by language, cultural tradition, perceptual framework, values, practical manners and the hierarchy of Western practices. Von Senger adds that Chinese has its own 'encoded eye', of which everyone, in transcultural communication, must be aware. This limitation on doing indigenous research in one's native land is also pointed out in the methodology of anthropological fieldwork. To overcome this weakness, as Feuchtwang suggests, we can, through self-reflection and self-description, try to distance ourselves as far as possible from the society in which we are embedded.

Fei Xiaotong's contributions to Chinese social science vocabularies and the globalization of knowledge

The articles published in this issue largely relate to Fei Xiaotong's book *From the Soil* (1992; *Xiangtu Zhongguo*, 1947). They have been sorted in the order suggested by the ever-larger circles in Fei's term '*chaxugeju*' (differential mode of association, or social egoism). This sequence starts with the vocabulary of anthropology as the signal discipline, then expands to social science methodology and theory and finally moves to the globalization of knowledge from a Chinese perspective, including Chinese culture and Chinese thought from both Chinese and non-Chinese scholars.

The first article is 'Fei Xiaotong and the vocabulary of anthropology in China', by Steven Harrell. This was originally presented at the Annual Meeting of the American Ethnological Society in 1997, and has been updated and first published in this issue. In his article, Harrell puts forward a series of thought-provoking methodological and philosophical questions. 'Have anthropologists in countries outside the Euro–American metropole been able to develop their own vocabulary, relatively free from the influence of Euro–American anthropology, in order to elucidate phenomena that, in their judgment, English (or French or German) terms do not fit? In other words, does Chinese anthropology have Chinese terms for concepts that are peculiar to Chinese society or other societies that Chinese anthropologists study? How well has this vocabulary fared? How much of their own specific vocabulary do non-metropolitan anthropologists need – what mix between borrowed or translated terms and native ones?' Perhaps this can be interpreted as a kind of 'transcultural generativity' (Yu's term).

Through reading *From the Soil*, Harrell discovered that Fei Xiaotong invented a series of words, such as *xiangtu shehui, tuantigeju, chaxugeju, jiazu* and *lizhi*. After studying them, Harrell concluded that *From the Soil (Xiangtu Zhongguo)* 'is a landmark for the indigenization of anthropology in non-Europhone countries and cultures, in that it begins the process of creating a technical anthropological vocabulary in the Chinese language'[6]. Although Harrell has a different opinion on the theoretical contribution of Fei's book from that of its translator, he believes some ideas and thoughts raised by Fei in the book need further study. This is particularly important, according to Harrell, as China is one of a few countries that have moved from peripheral to central status in the world system, and intellectual developments in China are becoming more and more difficult for the rest of the scholarly world to ignore.

Another article related to Fei Xiaotong's work and published here is '*Moulüe* (谋略 Supraplanning): on the problem of the transfer of earthbound words and concepts in the context of cultural exchange between China and the West', by Harro von Senger. He is keen to capture vocabularies that have methodological implications from Fei Xiaotong's writings and apply them to his studies on other issues, such as, in this case, *moulüe*. As early as 1995, von Senger published an article entitled 'Earthbound China – earthbound sinology'[7]. In it, von Senger proposed an 'earthbound Western' problem. He read *From the Soil (Xiangtu Zhongguo)* in both English and Chinese, but he was not influenced by the English translation. Instead, he directly quoted the original phrase from Fei Xiaotong that 'words are the most important bridges', and applied it methodologically to his study. With regard to the matter of translation of *moulüe* into English, according to von Senger, both Chinese and American translators lost its 'earthboundness' when they used the English words 'strategy' or 'stratagem', because they simply replaced a Chinese character with a superficially corresponding Western word with a much narrower meaning. The pre-existing Western word does not function as a 'bridge' (Fei's term) but as an 'artificial limb'. Von Senger believes that this kind of Westernization of a Chinese term creates an *illusion* of mutual understanding but does not lead to a *real* mutual understanding.

Moreover, for von Senger, there are two approaches to translating complicated Chinese characters into English. One is directly using pinyin, such as *moulüe* or *guanxi*, but the problem is that people still need to define such foreign words. Another approach is to make a new word, just as Feuchtwang coined 'social egoism' for *chaxugeju*. Such a new vocabulary is easier to understand and to use compared

---

[6] If you read Fei Xiaotong's *Peasant Life in China* (1939), you will remember that Malinowski wrote in his Preface that 'I venture to foretell that *Peasant Life in China* by Dr Hsiao-Tung Fei will be counted as a landmark in the development of anthropological fieldwork and theory' (Fei 1939: xix).

[7] It was borrowed from the title of Fei Xiaotong's early work (Hsiao-t'ung, Fei, & Chih-I, Chang. 1948. *Earthbound China: A Study of Rural Economy in Yunnan*. London: Routledge & Kegan Paul, 1948).

with 'the differential mode of association' of Hamilton's direct translation. Therefore, von Senger coined an English word, 'supraplanning', for *moulüe*. This way of translating difficult Chinese characters maintains their earthboundness, namely their original touch and meaning, and can be understood and may even be of practical use in the other cultural environment. This is particularly important in practice, as we see from a Chinese saying, 'Bite phrases and chew characters' (*yao wen jiao zi*), literally meaning to be excessively particular about wording). As a sinologist and lawyer, von Senger himself benefited from such 'chewing and nibbling' on moulüe, which can be seen in his interpretations of the *Constitution of the Communist Party of China*, *Law of the People's Republic of China on Chinese–Foreign Joint Ventures*, and China's policy towards the cross-strait relations between China and Taiwan, etc. Readers may find basic principles as well as useful and practical tips on understanding China's laws and policy in von Senger's article.

In 'What Western social scientists can learn from the writings of Fei Xiaotong', by Gary Hamilton, the main translator of Fei's *From the Soil*, the author tells us that in 1984 when he first read *Xiangtu Zhongguo*, he was trying to understand and describe the differences between *xiao* (孝filial piety) and *patria potestas* (家父权), which involves a comparison between traditional Chinese and Roman societies. Among many Western scholars, the most notable person to engage with such a comparison in the field was Max Weber. 'Weber argued that patriarchalism in China was the same phenomenon, typologically, as patriarchalism in the Mediterranean basin during Antiquity.' Hamilton sensed that Weber had made a serious semantic error when he equated them. Hamilton decided that not only did the pair of concepts *chaxugeju* and *tuantigeju*[8] that Fei invented contain profound insights into the nature of Chinese society, but his 'ideal–typical contrast between Chinese and Western societies also points the way to a new understanding of Western society'. Therefore, Hamilton corrected Weber's error[9] by observing that *patria potestas* is emblematic of a legitimating principle that empowers people to act within the bounds of their own jurisdictions, which is the same as Fei's *tuantigeju*; whereas *xiao* identifies a doctrine that obligates people to submit to the duties of their own roles, the principle of which is the same as Fei's *chaxugeju*. Hamilton cites as evidence a series of his own empirical studies that are supportive of his view.

Compared with many Western scholars' comparisons between *xiao* and *patria potestas*, Hamilton's comparative studies are obviously more convincing. However, Hamilton seems to have exaggerated the importance of xiao (filial piety)

---

[8] Hamilton and Wang translated *chaxugeju* and *tuantigeju* as a 'differential mode of association' and 'organizational mode of association', respectively.

[9] This was confirmed by Professor Wolfgang Schluchter at the international conference 'Max Weber and China: Culture, Law and Capitalism', held at SOAS, University of London, 5–6 September 2013 (http://www.ccpn-global.com/cms.php?artid=520&catid=63).

in the Chinese social and cultural context. Chinese parents have always embedded their expectations of their children in their names. The first character of Fei's first name is *xiao*, which also has the meaning of 'filial piety'. However, Fei himself never treated *xiao* as a vital term for understanding the Chinese social structure and political system. In fact, Fei made it very clear in *From the Soil* that it is a set of morals and ethics as an assurance mechanism that maintains *chaxugeju*, and *xiao* is just one of them (Fei 1985: 29–35). Furthermore, to contrast the conventional view of Western society as having 'a rule of law' (法治) and Chinese society as 'a rule of man' (人治), Fei invented another term, 'rule of ritual' (礼治), to describe Chinese society (48–53). The different emphasis shows that Fei's core theories have yet to be fully understood and recognized by Western scholarship. This is perhaps why Hamilton was surprised that his huge efforts in translating Fei into English had little impact in the West.

After reading the above translated version of *From the Soil*, Stephan Feuchtwang wrote 'Social egoism and individualism: surprises and questions from a Western anthropologist of China: reading Professor Fei Xiaotong's contrast between China and the West'. This paper was initially written for a conference celebrating the 70th anniversary of the beginning of Fei Xiaotong's academic career and the 20th anniversary of the Institute of Sociology and Anthropology at Peking University in 2005. It could never have existed in a world if there were no Chinese social scientific ritual to form a part of its methodology. And it could not be brought into mainstream academic discourse in the English-speaking world without JCCP as a platform.

In this article, Feuchtwang translated Fei Xiaotong's pair of concepts *chaxugeju* and *tuantigeju* as 'social egoism' and 'corporatism', respectively, thus enabling readers from the English-speaking world to place them within their own knowledge framework. Feuchtwang also made some comparative case studies, such as models of Fei Xiaotong vs Freedman, corporate group vs small lineage, Sage vs God, consensual power and what follows, changes in the study of kinship and the emotional family in China.

In addition, Feuchtwang highlights the importance of *From the Soil* by linking related issues to its subtitle, 'The Foundation of Chinese Society'. This can be seen from some of his thought-provoking questions, for example:

> If the Western countries moved from hierarchies of estates to individualist democracies under the same God, through republican revolutions, what happened to the status differentiation hierarchy of social persons after the republican revolutions in China? How was the social person the basis of a transformed Chinese politics and society? And: What was the effect in China of importing some of the ideals and politics of Western democracy and individualism?

Feuchtwang's translation of *chaxugeju* as social egoism was regarded by von Senger as a fine example of translating a difficult Chinese term into English. In his dialogue with me, Hamilton comments that translating *chaxugeju* as social egoism does not get at the interactional dimensions of Fei's concept. I agree with this point. According to Kerry Brown in a seminar for students of the MSc China in Comparative Perspective at LSE in 2012, Hamilton's translation of *From the Soil* and the concept of *chaxugeju* helped him to apply the Chinese characteristic network to an analysis of relationships among CPC senior party members, which distinguished his work (Hutton & Brown 2009) from others' on studies of the Community Party of China.

Understanding China's social sciences and its transcultural experiences in the process of the globalization of knowledge

In addition to the main articles, we introduce different forms of writing to focus on the main theme of this issue. This is the creation of vocabularies of social sciences from China in comparative perspective and the exploration of the structure of Chinese society and its operational mechanism in a global context. This issue publishes a version of the dialogue between Gary Hamilton and Xiangqun Chang, organized by an editor of the *China Reading Weekly*, China, to commemorate the 100th anniversary of the birth of Fei Xiaotong in 2010. In this dialogue, we discussed some reviews of *From the Soil*. One reviewer thought it was a waste of time to translate Fei's book, published in 1947, in the 1990s. It may therefore seem to some that it would be even more of a waste of time for us to spend a few issues discussing this in the 21st century. In the Editorial of the founding issue, I noted that one of JCCP's characteristics is to move through time and space. Some articles that were published in JCCP had been published in China a few years earlier, but had never been published in the West; yet they 'have wide-ranging significance: for the development of social science for those who come from a non-metropolitan society; also how knowledge may be attained in a globalizing world.'

Although eight of Fei Xiaotong's books[10] have been published in English, this is still less than one third of his total oeuvre, and, needless to say, three of them were published by a Chinese publisher. Two books that were republished by the University of Chicago Press had little impact on Western academia. In the dialogue, Chang explained that Fei Xiaotong wrote prolifically in the last 15 years of his life, concerning himself mostly with theory. Can we truly judge Fei's contribution without reading most of his work? Besides, even if readers in the West read Fei's English publications, how could they be sure they fully understood his work? Hamilton himself, who translated Fei's *From the Soil*, still overlooked one of the key points that Fei made about the assurance mechanism of *chaxugeju*. I include this example here not by any means as a criticism of

---

[10] See the eight books, cited in chronological order, in the References list. Note that Fei Xiaotong's publications appeared with four names: Fei Hsiao-Tung (Wade–Giles system), Fei Xiaotong (modern Chinese pinyin), 費孝通 (traditional Chinese characters), and 费孝通 (simplified Chinese characters).

Hamilton's scholarship, but to show how difficult it is to translate social science concepts and bring Chinese work to the West. That translation is central to the mission of JCCP and its parent, CCPN Global.

Furthermore, when the 'China model' was very topical after Joshua Cooper Ramo published *Beijing Consensus* in 2004, in both Chinese and Western discourse few works were able to link Fei Xiaotong's various models[11] with examining China's development model comprehensively and forging better understandings of its party policy or Chinese society and relationships with the rest of the world. This indicates that Chinese scholars also need to find ways to participate in the global discourse, especially as it relates to China. JCCP stitches related work from the past to the present, inside and outside China, and hopes to help readers to better understand China in the global context by introducing and interpreting the theoretical and methodological implications of Fei's work.

In her comments on the above-mentioned dialogue on Fei Xiaotong's contributions, Bettina Gransow said that she liked Hamilton's English version of *From the Soil*, as it made it much easier for her to discuss the 'Fei Xiaotong complex' in a class with students. Gransow senses the linkage between *chaxugeju* and *tuantigeju* and Fei's idea of the 'pattern of pluralist unity'. She pointed out the necessity of framing 'the entanglement of cultures in a dynamic pattern from a global perspective that takes into account that more and more people are living out of context (as Clifford Geertz once put it).'

Methodologically, the pros and cons of studying one's own native society have been of concern to Chinese scholars for decades. Gransow provides her answer to the question about the intrinsic advantages of studying one's own society. She makes it clear that Fei Xiaotong and his teacher Wu Wenzao at Peking University were aware of the fact that, in their fieldwork, they cared about and could affect the living conditions of their subjects, and that this was an intrinsic aspect of the work. Western scholars have not generally considered this extra dimension of Fei's work. But for Gransow,

> Fei's study represented an advance not only by virtue of examining a rural village (as part of a national context) as opposed to tribal societies, but also because it surely incorporated precisely the proximity between researcher and 'researchee' that Malinowki himself had never been able to generate in his own field research. Given his cultural distance to the 'natives' that formed his object of study, the method of participatory observation that he developed ran up against an insurmountable barrier.

In my dialogue with Hamilton, I revealed my understandings from reading Fei's completed work (2009). In the last two papers of his life, Fei repeatedly stressed

---

[11] e.g. the Southern Jiangsu Model, the Wenzhou Model or the Pearl River Model (Chang 2014: 7–13).

that the order of Chinese civilization is based on *li*-centred Confucian culture. Fei believed this philosophy of individual self-discipline promoted good social order.

This issue publishes two book reviews relating to *li*, both by YU Hua. These books are *Ritual and Deference* (Neville 2008) and *The Interweaving of Rituals* (Standaert 2008). In the first review, Yu points out that 'Neville understands Xunzi's concept of ritual as conventional signs that lie along a broad spectrum, almost permeating every sphere of social, political and private life.' Yu agrees with the statement that ritual (*li*) is the determinate fabric of Chinese culture and, further, it defines social political order (Hall & Ames 1998). From a practical perspective, Yu found Neville's critical interpretation of the war launched by some American Christians on Muslim nations to be based on their material interests, so he sought Confucius' ritual and its embedded humane values as a possible solution:

> Good rituals make civilized life possible. Without good rituals, no matter what the intent or how good the will of people with different interests, civilized life is impossible.

YU Hua's second book review on funerals, in the cultural exchange between China and Europe, resonates with Shuo Yu's article on transcultural generativity in China–Europe encounters. In the book review, YU reports that Standaert explores the integration, controversy, hybridization and amalgamation of different cultures by presenting missionaries' and Chinese converts' texts on death rituals.

The author first weaves two pieces of 'solid-coloured' cloth by sketching out the funeral in China and Europe respectively before the two cultures' encounter. In Chapter One, he elaborates on the orthodox Confucian death ritual and the popular practice that integrated Buddhists and Taoists, presenting the Chinese death rites as a piece of cloth that has already been interwoven with a warp and weft of Buddhism and Daoism.

If readers are interested in details, I suggest they read the original work by Standaert. I would like to add that, in his *Introduction to Death Ritual in Late Imperial and Modern China* (Watson & Rawski 1988), Watson argues that the 'Chinese state had no effective means of controlling beliefs regarding the afterlife' (p. 11). My book on *Guanxi or li shang wanglai* backs up the idea that the death ritual and other kinds of rituals (*li*) are a key to understanding how Chinese society operates.

> The above question was asked by Watson in the days before the June 4th Event in 1989[12], in 'studies of Chinese funerals' (Watson 1988:3). Since then, socialist regimes in the USSR and Eastern Europe fell from power like dominoes whilst the Chinese government steadfastly stood its ground under economic sanctions by many major Western countries. The question of 'What holds Chinese society

---

[12] The English version of my book failed to be published in mainland China in 2009 because it mentioned the 'June 4th Event'.

together?' was raised again in the context of the economy, international relations and people interested in China and Chinese studies. The study of rural Chinese people's social support arrangements and *lishang-wanglai* reflected the above question from a different angle.' (Chang 2010: 539)

After conversations with many Chinese editors at the publishing house, I learnt that it was not just the 'June 4th Event' that cannot be mentioned. There was a fear of not understanding what I wrote in the entire English version, even when there was a Chinese version as a reference. There was also the matter of lack of linguistic ability, because they said that they knew how to correct my Chinese version but were unable to do English corrections in the same manner.

Finally, I move on to the Chinese for Social Sciences (CSS) column of this issue. JCCP, the dual-language journal, has four groups of readers in terms of languages: English readers, Chinese readers, professionals in China or outside China who want to gain comprehensive understandings of the same issue through checking dual languages, and non-Chinese who want to learn Chinese and Chinese who want to learn English in the context of social scientific studies on China. CSS consists of two sessions: reading and translation. They are written in Chinese by experienced linguists who have taught related courses in UK higher educational institutions.

The reading session includes intermediate and advanced levels. Apart from reading material, each piece contains some terms and phrases in Chinese with English explanations. The contents are derived from the same issue focusing on the same theme. For example, both 'Ripples and Straws' (intermediate level) by Lik Suen and 'A Chinese Map and a Raphael Fresco' (advanced level) by Lianyi Song are adapted from the article 'What Western social scientists can learn from the writings of Fei Xiaotong' by Gary Hamilton. The material and questions are a helpful aid for reading and understanding the original article.

The translation session includes Chinese to English and English to Chinese. Certain English sentences or small paragraphs are provided as samples for analysis. 'Translation of Philosophy and Philosophy of Translation: Social Science Translation' (by Dongning Feng) is based on two book reviews. According to Feng, Confucius' *ren* is commonly translated as 'humaneness' and 'good'. The 'good' is similar to Plato's 'idea of the good' or 'form of the good', but it is different from Western philosophical usage, which is an abstract concept, whereas *ren* has a clear meaning. For Feng, *ren* can be translated into English thus:

> kindness, benevolence, goodness, compassion, social conscience, charity, charitableness, humanity, philanthropism, generosity, magnanimity, liberality, beneficence. However, none of these could grasp the elements of *ren* in the following ways, such as 孝 (filial piety), 悌 (respect for elder brothers), 忠 (loyalty), 恕 (sympathy), 礼 (ritual / etiquette), 知 (knowledge), 勇 (gallantry), 恭 (humility), 宽 (generosity), 信 (honesty), 敏 (diligence), 惠 (charity) and so on.

This example shows how difficult it can be to properly convey the meaning of a single Chinese character to English speakers. The *Journal of China in Comparative Perspective* (JCCP) provides a space in which to make intellectual bricks with words, vocabularies, ideas... to build a palace of human knowledge wherein global issues can be tackled with the aim of building a harmonious, mutually understanding global society.

To conclude: on the one hand, the *Journal of China in Comparative Perspective* (JCCP) produces high-quality academic and intellectual products, including articles and book reviews and other publications; on the other hand, it works with CCPN Global, which encourages interdisciplinary, inter-institutional, transnational and comparative approaches, and facilitates collaborative studies on China in its Asian and global contexts. The results of our research and any consequent policy outcomes will feed back into our publications as global public goods, to serve the global academic community and make the benefits available to society worldwide.

References

Albrow, Martin. 1987. Sociology for One World. *International Sociology*. Vol. 2:1-12.

— 1991. Internationalism as a Publication Project: Experience in Editing an International Sociological Journal. *Current Sociology*. Vol. 39: 101-18.

常向群主编.2014.《社会建设: 中国社会发展的一种模式》.徐海燕等编译, 伦敦: 全球中国出版社。

— 2015.《社会建设: 中国社会发展的一种模式》.徐海燕等编译, 北京: 新世界出版社与伦敦: 全球中国出版社合作出版。

— 2004.《关系抑或礼尚往来? 江村互惠、社会支持网和社会创造的研究》.英国城市大学社会学系博士论文。

— 2009. 年. 关系抑或礼尚往来? 江村互惠、社会支持网和社会创造的研究》.中文简体字版, 毛明华译, 辽宁人民出版社。

— 2010. 年.《關係抑或禮尚往來? —江村互惠、社會支持網和社會創造的研究》(繁体字版).毛明华翻译, 李孟珊 润校, 台灣華藝學術出版公司。

Chang, Xiangqun. ed. 2015. *Society Building: A China Model of Social Development* (new edition). London: Global China Press and Beijing: New World Press.

— ed. 2014. *Society Building: A China Model of Social Development*. Newcastle upon Tyne: Cambridge Scholars Publishing.

— 2010. *Guanxi or Li shang wanglai?: Reciprocity, Social Support Networks & Social Creativity in a Chinese Village*. Taipei: Scholarly Publishing Business, Airiti Press, Inc.

Cuccioletta, Donald. 2001/2002. 'Multiculturalism or transculturalism: towards a cosmopolitan citizenship'. *London Journal of Canadian Studies* 17.

Fei Hsiao-tung (Fei Xiaotong). 1939. *Peasant Life in China. A Field Study of Country Life in the Yangtze Valley*. New York: E. P. Dutton & Company.

— & Chang Chih-I. 1945. *Earthbound China: A Study of Rural Economy in Yunnan*. London: Routledge & Kegan Paul.

— 1953. *China's Gentry: Essays in Rural–Urban Relations*. Ed and revised by Margaret Park Redfield. Chicago and London: University of Chicago Press.

— 1981. *Toward a People's Anthropology*. Beijing: New World Press.

— 1983. *Chinese Village Close-up*. Beijing: New World Press.

— et al. 1986. *Small Towns in China: Functions, Problems & Prospects*. Beijing: New World Press.

— 1989. *Rural Development in China: Prospect and Retrospect* (portions of this book were originally published by NWP in the above two books in 1983 and 1986, with a Foreword by Tang Tsou). Chicago and London: University of Chicago Press.

— 1992. *From the Soil: The Foundations of Chinese Society*. A translation of Fei Xiaotong's *Xiangtu Zhongguo* with an introduction and an epilogue by Gary Hamilton and Wang Zheng. Berkeley, CA: University of California Press

— *Globalization and Cultural Self-Awareness* [a collection of Fei's writings], ed. Lili Fang. 2015. Berlin and Heidelberg: Springer.

费孝通. 2009.《费孝通全集》. (20卷), 呼和浩特: 内蒙古人民出版社 [(Fei Xiaotong. 2009. Fei Xiaotong Quanji (Fei Xiaotong Completed Works) (20 vols). Hohhot: Inner Mongolia People's Publishing House.

—《江村经济—中国农民的生活》.1986.戴可景译.南京: 江苏人民出版社。

— 1985.《乡土中国》.北京: 三联书店([1947]. *Xiangtu Zhongguo* (in Chinese), Beijing: SDX Joint Publishing Company.

费孝通著. 2013.《全球化与文化自觉: 费孝通晚年文选》.方李莉编, 北京: 外语教学与研究出版社。

王斯福、常向群、周大鸣. 2015.《中国社会科学全球化 — 费孝通诞辰一百周年论文集》, 北京: 新世界出版社和伦敦: 全球中国出版社合作出版

Feuchtwang, S., Chang, X., & Zhou, D. 2015. *Globalization of Chinese Social Science: Commemorating the 100th Anniversary of Professor Fei Xiaotong's Birth*. London: Global China Press and Beijing: New World Press.

Flüchter, Antje, & Schöttli, Jivanta. eds. 2015. *The Dynamics of Transculturality: Concepts and Institutions in Motion*. Berlin and Heidelberg: Springer.

Hepp, Andreas. 2009. 'Transculturality as a perspective: researching media cultures comparatively'. *Forum: Qualitative Social Research* 10(1).

Hutton, Will, & Brown, Kerry. 2009. *Friends and Enemies: The Past, Present and Future of the Communist Party of China (China in the 21st Century)*. London and New York: Anthem Press.

Lewis, Jeff. 2002. 'From culturalism to transculturalism'. *Iowa Journal of Cultural Studies* 1.

Schachtner, Christina. 2015. 'Transculturality in the internet: culture flows and virtual publics'. *Current Sociology* 63: 228–243.

Slimbach, Richard. 2005. 'The transcultural journey'. *Frontiers: The Interdisciplinary Journal of Study Abroad* 11.

苏新宁主编. 2007.《中国人文社会科学学术影响力报告 (2000–2004)》, 北京:中国社会科学出版社。[Xinning, Su. ed. 2007. *A Report on the Academic Influence of the Research Achievements in Humanities and Social Sciences in China (2000–2004)*. Beijing: China Social Science Publishing House.]

Welsch, Wolfgang. 1999. 'Transculturality: the puzzling form of cultures today'. In Mike Featherstone and Scott Lash, eds. *Spaces of Culture: City, Nation, World*. London: Sage.

Yunxiang Yan. 1996. *The Flow of Gifts: Reciprocity and Social Networks in a Chinese Village*. Redwood City, CA: Stanford University Press.

阎云翔. 1999.《礼物的流动: 一个中国村庄中的互惠原则与社会网络》. 李放春, 刘瑜翻译, 上海:上海人民出版社。

翟学伟. 2006.《社会事实再现的文学路径--建构社会与行为科学中的人文方法》.《社会理论论丛》第3辑, 南京大学出版社。[Xuewei, Zhai. 2006. 'Representing social facts by a literary path: a humanity methodology in the construction of society and human behaviours'. *Social Theory* 3. Nanjing: Nanjing University Press.]

DOI https://doi.org/10.24103/GCSS1.en.2015.3

Fei Xiaotong and the Vocabulary
of Anthropology in China

Stevan Harrell

Abstract: Fei Xiaotong's series of essays, based on his lectures on 'Rural Sociology', was published in the 1940s as *Xiangtu Zhongguo*. It is a landmark for the indigenization of anthropology in non-Europhone countries and cultures, in that it begins the process of creating a technical anthropological vocabulary in the Chinese language. Fei, having obtained his doctorate at the London School of Economics, understood clearly the English-language vocabulary of anthropology, and thereby understood where that vocabulary was and was not appropriate to understanding Chinese society. He realized that direct translation of English terms into Chinese could sometimes create confusion and misunderstanding, and so in addition to using conventional Chinese translations of English terms, he invented a series of new Chinese terms he considered more appropriate to the analysis of Chinese society. Unfortunately, the Communist Revolution interrupted Fei's indigenization project, superimposing translations of terms from the Marxist ethnological tradition developed in the Soviet Union. Today, however, as anthropology everywhere outside Euro-America continues its quest to indigenize, Fei's early attempt at indigenization can serve as a partial guide to creating an appropriate anthropological vocabulary in Chinese, and perhaps as an example for how to create such a vocabulary in other languages.

Keywords: vocabulary, translation, indigenization, anthropology, China

I often remark to graduate students in anthropology, and not entirely facetiously, that the way to make a name for yourself in our pre- or non-paradigmatic science is to name something else, to invent a term. Having done the thickest ethnographic description in the world pales in importance before having first used the word 'liminality' or 'traveling theory' or even 'thick description.' A term has to stick, of course, and one can be judged to have had one's term stick when it gets cited in a tertiary mode, particularly if it earns the classifier 'notion,' or even better, 'concept' as in 'Jo Schmo uses Bourdieu's concept of cultural capital to look at...'. Here Jo Schmo has done all right, but Pierre Bourdieu has arrived. In other words, a case can be made that our discipline, our discourse, revolves around vocabulary.

It can be argued that as long as anthropology is practiced in a world of unequal power relations (Said, 1978), *theories* developed in the metropole are inherently prejudicial to *practice* that increasingly emanates from the periphery. Anthropology is tainted with colonial and neo-colonial aims, personnel, and theoretical arguments. I think this is true, and I think that the survival of the discipline in the next fifty years probably depends on our being able to come up with a satisfactory answer to the question of whether our discourse is inherently colonial or Eurocentric, and thus will pass with the passing of the colonial and Eurocentric world order just as scholasticism passed with the Reformation and Counter-Reformation, or Neo-Confucian *lixue* (理学) passed with the May 4th movement, or whether we can develop a multilateral or decentered discourse that will still speak to important questions in the world order of our grandchildren.

As China continues its 'peaceful rise' and its effort to reassume what its leaders assume is its *deserved* place in the international company of nations, the question of how Chinese scholars are approaching the problem of de-colonializing or de-Eurocenticizing the social sciences takes on added importance. China is one of the few countries that has moved from peripheral to central status in the world system, and as this happens, intellectual developments in China are becoming more and more difficult for the rest of the scholarly world to ignore.

Perhaps ironically, however, as Chinese intellectual life becomes more relevant to the rest of the world, and as the Chinese government continues its push to get the world to learn Chinese, through Confucius Institutes all over the world and through generous scholarship opportunities for foreign students, foreign languages are getting less attention in the United Kingdom and other countries, and authorities there have raised the alarm that there is 'a decline in modern language learning' (British Academy, 2009). And nowhere is the knowledge of language more important than in the social sciences, which are not built on mathematical concepts but on linguistic ones.

If, as I suggested above, the discipline of anthropology revolves around vocabulary, then we can see readily how the role of vocabulary in anthropology provides a more specific context in which to address the general questions of China and the role of language in our contemporary world. We know, of course, that in the early years of anthropology (say until the 1960s), the vocabulary of our discipline was overwhelmingly English-language vocabulary (with a considerable dollop of French thrown in, and a tiny pinch of German), even when the practitioners were natives of the countries that usually formed the object of anthropological research (even Jomo Kenyatta used English to write *Facing Mount Kenya* (1938), and certainly Talal Asad used English to write and edit *Anthropology and the Colonial Encounter* (1973). But there have been exceptions from early on, and these exceptions increase as various former object countries, including notably those in the Sinophone world, develop anthropological discourses of their own, and of course are faced with translating the vocabulary and concepts of anthropology into a host of languages.

There are two kinds of question about the vocabulary of anthropology in languages other than those of the discipline's founders. One concerns translation: as theorists of translation have emphasized from the beginning, words don't match in different languages, or else translation would be a mechanical exercise (see Steiner, 1975; Schulte and Biguenet, 1992). 'Community,' '*Gemeinschaft*,' '*kyoodootai*共同体' and '*shequ*社区,' although they are 'standard' translations of each other, do not mean the same thing.   The fact that the referents of these terms overlap but do not coincide influences the way the corresponding *concepts* will evolve differently as they appear in the anthropologies written in the different languages.   As a frequent translator of Chinese-language anthropological writings into English, I realize this acutely, and have even written on what the most appropriate English translation for a term like *minzu* (民族) might be[1] (2001: 29-48).   When on rare occasions I have tried to write anthropology in Chinese, I encounter two additional questions: Do I really think in different concepts when I write in Chinese, and when I translate my own Chinese into my native English, how close is the result to what I would have written had I composed the piece in English in the first place (Harrell and Li, 2011; Harrell, 2002)?   These were certainly questions that Professor Fei must have faced when he wrote *Xiangtu Zhongguo* in Chinese (1948) and *Peasant Life in China* (1939) in English. All of them are practical questions which in addition have theoretical and philosophical reverberations far beyond anthropology.

On a slightly less practical level, how well do translated terms used in anthropology resonate with their linguistic environment, which we can assume in most cases to be the elite, intellectual discourse in their various communities? Are there differences between the ordinary use of the terms and their anthropological use? Do they introduce concepts that are alien to, or somehow don't seem to fit with, the conceptual universe, the ordinary intellectual vocabulary, commonly used in that language? Do they force anthropologists working in that language to use concepts alien to that broader intellectual community, and if so does this alienate the anthropologists from that community, or make their writings inaccessible to others outside the discipline? *Muxi Shehui* (母系社会) is certainly a clear Chinese translation of the English *matrilineal society*, but it means something different in a society where people are taught from childhood that matriliny is a primitive state that we all shared in the past, even though most anthropologists in China have recently rejected the antiquated Morganian paradigm of social evolution.

Or perhaps we are being too negative here.   Perhaps borrowed and/or translated vocabulary can be turned to appropriately native ends, and borrowed or translated terms can be turned to more native referents, shedding new light on local phenomena. As an example, the Chinese term *tuteng* (图腾), which is not even a translation, but a direct borrowing of an English (actually Algonkian) term, *totem*, does not seem to have the baggage in Chinese that it has acquired in the Anglo-French world with its genealogy from Rivers (1909) to Radcliffe-Brown (1929) to Lévi-Strauss (1962), and can be used in a rather more simple and

---

[1] There isn't really a good one: see Harrell, 2001: 29-48.

straightforward sense of an animal or plant that stands metonymically for a people or an ethnic group.

Or there is still another possibility to consider, which is the main topic of this article: have anthropologists in countries outside the Euro-American metropole been able to develop their own vocabulary, relatively free from the influence of Euro-American anthropology, in order to elucidate phenomena that, in their judgment, English (or French or German) terms do not fit? In other words, does Chinese anthropology have Chinese terms for concepts that are peculiar to Chinese society or other societies that Chinese anthropologists study? How well has this vocabulary fared? How much of their own specific vocabulary do non-metropolitan anthropologists need – what mix between borrowed or translated terms and native ones?

This is a broad topic in the history of Chinese anthropology, and before delving into what we can learn about it from studying Professor Fei's writings, here I want to mention a few other areas of the intellectual history of anthropology in China that bear on these questions.

First, why and how did Chinese social scientists in the early 20th century almost completely abandon traditional ethnological concepts? Beginning with the *Xinan Yi Liezhuan* 《西南夷列传》 of Sima Qian's *Shi Ji* (司马迁《史记》) in the second century B.C.E., and continuing into the mid-Qing period, Chinese officials and scholars wrote accounts of the peoples on China's peripheries. These were not merely descriptive, but also employed generalizing theoretical concepts, such as the difference between *sheng* (生) and *shu* (熟) (strange and familiar, or beyond and within the influence of civilization, an idea similar to those embodied in the cultural evolutionism of both bourgeois and Marxist ethnology), the general process of *guihua* (归化), or assimilation, and how it worked, and a kind of ecological determinism, similar to that employed by late 19th-century Euro-American theorists, correlating certain types of character and morals with farming, herding, and other subsistence pursuits. Yet when we find anthropology emerging in China in the 1920s, the leaders all attached themselves to one or another school of European origin, such as German *Kulturkreislehre* or British Social Anthropology's structural-functionalism. Why, in developing an anthropological discourse of their own, did Chinese scholars reject traditional concepts almost entirely, and take up imported ones, rather than developing a synthesis? Why do we find, for example, in the works of Fei Xiaotong described below, much use of traditional aphorisms to describe specific phenomena, but no use of traditional theoretical terms or synthesizing categories?

Second, how did Marxist ethnology's concepts change or adapt as they were introduced into China? Here we need to bear in mind that for China (and also Vietnam) the Euro-American metropole has not been the only one exporting concepts (and in the context of this paper, vocabulary) to the periphery. As China began to import various kinds of bourgeois Euro-

American anthropological theory, starting with Cai Yuanpei's call for *minzuxue* (民族学) in the 1920s (Cai, 1962), it also imported a different canon, that of revolutionary Marxist social analysis. The revolution of 1949 forced Chinese anthropologists or ethnologists[2] to begin absorbing that other vocabulary, the words of the alternative, non-bourgeois ethnology that had been developed in the Soviet Union under Stalin. We can ask the same questions, *mutatis mutandis*, about China's importation of this vocabulary (whose immediate source language is, of course, Russian rather than English) as about the importation of Euro-American vocabulary: to what extent does it fit China and Chinese concerns or not, and within the general revolutionary Marxist discourse, has native vocabulary emerged, and in what sort of mix with translated or borrowed terms?

In particular we can put an anthropological twist on the question of whether Mao Zedong's greatly touted 'sinification of Marxism' (Wylie, 1979; Knight, 1990) was really a move toward a Marxist version of a synthesis between European and local concepts and vocabulary, or even whether Mao's early analysis of Chinese society was a native anthropological discourse, albeit an applied revolutionary one? It is well known that Mao, when he wrote some of his early works such as *Zhongguo Shehui Ge Jieji de Fenxi* (《中国社会各阶级的分析》) in 1925, and the scarily magnificent *Hunan Nongmin Yundong Kaocha Baogao* (《湖南农民运动考察报告》) in 1927, was not well acquainted even with what Marxist theory and terminology were available in Chinese at the time (he never learned any other language), and that the Hunan report was considered quite unorthodox by his comrades. In addition, by the time he wrote his famous 'liberal' pieces of 1956 and 1957, *Lun Shi Da Guanxi* (《论十大关系》) and *Guanyu Zhengque Chuli Renmin Neibu Maodun de Wenti* (《关于正确处理人民内部矛盾的问题》), he was dissatisfied with orthodoxy, particularly imported orthodoxy, for other reasons. An analysis of the language in these pieces would provide an idea of whether and how China might have developed an indigenous Marxist anthropological vocabulary.

Third, to what extent has Chinese anthropological vocabulary, imported, borrowed, translated or otherwise, affected the discourse on minority peoples and on ethnic differences in today's China? It seems to me that if Chinese anthropological vocabulary is derivative from Western and Russian languages, then any discourse about minority peoples must involve a double-layered linguistic removal from fact, using Chinese-language terms that themselves have been borrowed or translated, and to use them to describe a local minority reality that is understood by its participants in a language unrelated to Chinese (because no language is closely related to Chinese). In a few cases of ethnology written in the minority languages, the terms themselves are borrowed twice, or perhaps translated and then borrowed or translated twice (I don't think they would be

---

[2] Few of whom had originally had much sympathy with Marxism, though many supported the revolution for humanitarian reasons.

borrowed and then translated, but I may be wrong). Reflection on this question would allow us to mix the syntagm of two-layered colonial influence with the paradigm comparing Chinese discourses about minorities either to cosmopolitan discourses about China or to discourses about minority peoples (such as Native Americans) in the metropolitan countries.

All these topics would have to be included in a comprehensive treatment of Chinese anthropological vocabulary, but in this issue, dedicated to the anthropological legacy of Fei Xiaotong, I want to concentrate on a fourth one, on what I see as, with the possible exception of some of Mao's early unorthodox writings, the earliest attempt to create a modern native anthropological vocabulary in China, as embodied in Fei's 1948 essay collection, *Xiangtu Zhongguo.*

Fei's book has been ably translated into English by Gary Hamilton and Wang Zheng as *From the Soil: The Foundations of Chinese Society* (1992). In their introduction, Hamilton and Wang discuss the novelty, even uniqueness of this work: they call it 'Fei Xiaotong's first and only effort to construct a non-Western theoretical foundation for a sociology of Chinese society,' and even go so far as to claim that this work 'represents one of the few and certainly one of the most insightful efforts to build a sociology of a non-Western society' (1992: 4) They also point out that it contains 'an implicit criticism of foreign theories applied to China' (1992: 18) It is not, of course, an effort totally *de novo*, and in fact the foreign elements in Fei's analysis probably balance or slightly outweigh the innovative ones. But what is significant (and this is pointed out clearly in Hamilton and Wang's introduction) is that Fei, despite his impeccable English education at the feet of the great Malinowski and others, simply refuses to apply foreign-derived concepts or terms uncritically to China. He uses them where he sees them fit, and invents new ones of his own where they don't fit, always patiently explaining why he has to depart from the conventions of Euro-American derived theory.

Except where they insist on claiming him as a sociologist (in the 1940s, at least, he was good enough on our anthropology team, and after all his English-language mentors included both Redfield and Malinowski), I don't wish to contest or attack any element of Hamilton and Wang's analysis of Fei's work. What I do propose to do (ironically, since they actually translated it and all I did was read it and take notes) is to give more explicit public attention than they do to the role of vocabulary in Fei's book, to consider his quasi-nativist achievement in light of my general questions about importation and invention of vocabulary. To do so, I will point out some of the instances in which Fei uses new or newly redefined vocabulary to express ideas about Chinese society that he considers unreachable by conventional English-language terminology, pointing out how he uses them and how he explains their usage. In each case, I will then go on to show how Hamilton and Wang's translation (back) into English, the metropolitan language of sociology and anthropology, illustrates in a looking-glass way some of the problems that Fei himself faced when learning anthropology in English and trying to apply it to China, and some of the reasons why he had to come up with neologisms.

Fei's Argument and the Role of Neologisms

The first and most important indication that Fei is no slave to his British education comes in the first few paragraphs of his book, which are heavy in multiple uses of the term *tu* (土) and compounds formed with *tu*. Fei begins by saying that Chinese society is basically *xiangtuxing de* (乡土性的), in English (very) roughly 'local' or perhaps 'rural' or even 'village-based'. He then goes on to say that we should pay attention to those *bei chengwei tutou tunao de xiangxiaren* (被称为土头土脑 的乡下人), again roughly, rural people who are called *tu*-headed and *tu*-brained. And in the next paragraph, he points out that rural people are often said to have *tuqi* (土气) or a *tu* aura, perhaps, while on the next page he refers to the fact that in the countryside (*xiangxia* 乡下) *tu* is the root of their existence (*tamen de ming gen* 他们的命根). And finally, the preeminence of the earth deity, *tudi* (土地), is due to the fact that it symbolizes *kegui de nitu* (可贵的泥土), that valuable *tu*. All of these expressions use the term *tu* in somewhat different ways. Hamilton and Wang, for example, translate *xiangtuxing de* as 'rural;' *bei chengwei tutou tunao de xiangxiaren* as 'those so called hayseeds living in the countryside,' and *tuqi* as 'soiled,' though they are unsure enough of the last to include the original *tuqi* in parentheses in the English text. *Tu* as the root of existence is translated as soil. *Tudi* is named in Chinese and then glossed as god of the earth, and finally, *nitu* as the earth itself. So in English, we have rural, hayseed, soil, and earth, a group of terms that certainly have mutual resonances, but nothing like the unity of the cluster of terms all built out of the three simple strokes of the character *tu*.

Although I have given my own rather intuitive translations of the terms above, while leaving *tu* untranslated for the time being, I have no reason to quibble with any of Hamilton and Wang's translations, except that I would prefer 'hick' to 'hayseed,' even though neither one has dirt or earth or soil or ground in it. My point here is that Fei is introducing, as his fundamental term referring to the whole social complex he wishes to analyze, a term that *must* be in Chinese, that cannot have been derived from any European language, because European languages do not have this resonating cluster of meanings built on the same root, a resonance that washes out when even the best of translators try to put it into a European language. And Fei is not just describing something here; he is introducing a new anthropological concept of *xiangtu shehui* (乡土社会) which, by including multiple different resonances of *tu*, is much richer and more multivalent than any possible English equivalent, even though the second part of the compound (*shehui*) is a Chinese transpronunciation of a two-character term invented in Meiji Japan as a rough equivalent of the Western society, *societé*, or *Gesellschaft*. The distinction Fei makes between *xiangtu* and urban (nothing remarkable in his translation of that term) is not the same as Raymond Williams's country and city

(1973), for example, and it does not say the same things about the countryside as are embedded in the orthodox Chinese Communist term *nongcun* (农村), a term that implies a kind of technological determinism absent from Fei's work, but that Fei does not use once in his entire book.

The distinction between *xiangtu* and something else (which varies from *dushi* (都市) or urban, to *xifang* (西方) or *xiyang* (西洋, 'Western'), is the root of several other dichotomies Fei constructs in his book, each of which is a corresponding binary. The most famous of these, and the only one treated systematically by Hamilton and Wang in their introduction, is that between two different modes of social structure (for which Fei again uses a translated term, *shehui jiegou* 社会结构). These are the *tuantigeju* (团体格局) of Western or urban societies, and the *chaxugeju* (差序格局) of the *xiangtu* society. Hamilton and Wang point out that *chaxugeju* as a term is 'awkward in Chinese,' (1992 : 19-20) and surmise (correctly, I think) that Fei purposely used an awkward or unnatural term because he was trying to elucidate a concept for which there was no term either in the natural discourse of everyday intellectual Chinese or in the anthropological vocabulary imported from Europe and America. We do not need to go into a detailed exegesis of the terms here; it should suffice to point out that *geju*(格局) is a rather specialized-sounding term referring to an order of relationships or mode of distinction or categorization; Hamilton and Wang come up with 'mode of association,' and that should be good enough. *Tuanti*(团体), also adopted from the Japanese, refers to a social group, and Fei states that although Chinese often use this word to refer to any social collectivity, in the particular technical vocabulary that he is trying to invent, there are no *tuanti*, no bounded, hierarchically organized social groups in China's *xiangtu* society. There are, instead, person-centered networks based on a multiplicity of individual distinctions of rank and distance. It is these ranks and distances (*chaxu*差序) that shape the network of every Chinese individual.

It is interesting for us to note that Fei's concept of *chaxugeju*, while it is something that he invented in order to help explain Chinese *xiangtu* society to Chinese readers, in fact corresponds in many interesting ways both to the network analysis begun a decade or so later by Western anthropologists dissatisfied with the group-orientation of classical British structural-functionalism (Bott, 1957), and to the networks of personal obligation explored by outside and native analysis of Japan beginning with Benedict's *The Chrysanthemum and the Sword* (1946). But Fei was ahead of his British colleagues, and coeval with Benedict, whose work he was presumably not interested in since it is clear that he was only interested in China. So he invented network theory on his own. It wasn't unique to China like the whole complex built around *tu*, but it was nevertheless an independent invention of a Chinese anthropologist trying to explain Chinese society and finding borrowed or translated terms to be inadequate. In this case, it turned out to be applicable to a wide range of societies, though Fei rarely gets credit for inventing it and its practitioners for the most part don't acknowledge his contribution.

Another place where Fei feels he has to invent new vocabulary to question the validity of a Western-derived dichotomy is in reference to family and kinship. He begins (Fei, 1948: 39), by criticizing a distinction that he must have learned at London: between small and large family systems, or nuclear and extended family systems. He says that the whole notion of family (usually translated into Chinese as *jiating* (家庭)) belongs to the realm of *tuanti*, and so is inadequate to describe the small kin or household units of the *xiangtu* society. Instead, the relevant object to consider here is the *jiazu* (家族), a patrilineal kinship network whose ties lose strength as they become more distant from the individual, unlike a *jiating* whose boundaries are rigid and sociocentric. Who counts as an agnatic relative depends on who you are, in other words, and the term *jiating* simply doesn't fit.

Hamilton and Wang translate *jiazu* (家族) as patrilineage (chapter 6), and indeed this is a standard, uncontentious translation. But it masks, in a way, the distinction Fei is making between *jiazu* as an aspect of *chaxugeju* and *jiating* as an aspect of *tuantigeju*. This is because many Western students of China, beginning with Maurice Freedman (1958, 1966), the most canonical figure for the Western discourse on Chinese society, used terms such as lineage and patrilineage, but used them to construct a group-centered view of rural China, something Fei would consider an imposition of the *tuantigeju* model onto a society where it didn't belong. Fei's *jiazu* is not really Freedman's patrilineage. What is at issue here is not whether Fei or Freedman was right.[3] What is of interest is that, first, Fei saw the Western literature as inadequate for understanding the family in rural China, so he invented a new definition for the term *jiazu,* and second that Freedman, never having learned to read Chinese, missed out on a possible interpretation for his data. Freedman did have the English-language of Lin Yaohua (1948), but his works were written about Fujian; and of Hu Hsien-chin (1948), but hers was written as an English dissertation, less detached from or able to reflect on the European concepts than Fei was by the time he was writing *Xiangtu Zhongguo*.

Fei invented another potentially significant term, *lizhi* (礼治), in response to his dissatisfaction with the distinction between 'rule by law' and 'rule by men' in Western thinking, two concepts that commonly translated into Chinese rather conventionally as *fazhi* (法治) and *renzhi* (人治), respectively. Fei displays no problem with 'rule by law' or its Chinese translation, *fazhi,* in describing the Western or urban society contrasted to *xiangtu* society. Laws are definite rules that are laid down in a social contract and have to be followed. But he presents a devastating critique of the idea that either Confucian moral philosophy or the customary procedure of the *xiangtu* society constitutes rule by men, in the sense

---

[3]   I suspect part of the difference may have been due to Fei's roots in the Lake Tai region, combined with his fieldwork in Yunnan, as opposed to Freedman''s work in the land of the corporate patri-lineage in Fujian and Guangdong

that he understands, giving the right to decide to certain men and relying on their judgment. He points out that such authority is given to specific men only on the condition or assumption that they possess superior knowledge of *li* (礼), which he defines (using a mass of Western-derived terms) as *shehui gongren heshi de xingwei guifan* (社会公认合适的行为规范), which we might back-translate (rather awkwardly) as 'rules for behavior which are generally recognized by society as appropriate.' The way to understand *xiangtu* society is not as *renzhi*, which has much too great a connotation of arbitrariness or capriciousness, but as *lizhi* (礼治), ruled by convention or propriety. It is quite possible, and indeed justifiable in my opinion, that Fei felt insulted by what he considered an invidious distinction, but I read his analysis not so much as a reaction to an insult as a reaction to a misunderstanding, to a scholarly mistake.

The Significance of *Xiangtu Zhongguo*

These are not a lot of terms – *xiangtu shehui, chaxugeju, jiazu, lizhi*. But as I say to my students, all you have to do to become famous is to invent one. Fei, on the other hand, invented not so much four or five or eleven terms, as a whole complex of terminology which derives from an insider's dissatisfaction toward the outside terms he was handed in the unequal discourse between the Western anthropological canon and what he perceived as the Chinese reality. In *Xiangtu Zhongguo*, he was on his way to indigenizing anthropology in the best possible way – taking what seemed appropriate from the Euro-American discourse[4] and then inventing new, more appropriate terminology for those things that the Euro-American vocabulary either mislabeled or didn't address at all. This, I think, is enough that we should recognize the *brilliance* of Fei's achievement; it remains to speculate on its *significance*.

First, we might ask to what degree Fei's work could serve as a model for anthropologists in other non-metropolitan societies trying to indigenize their own anthropology. I see no reason why it could not be an important model, or one of a series of important models. Fei's sensitivity not only to the social conditions of China, but more importantly to the problems of translation and the particular relative strengths and weaknesses of English and Chinese, could be transferred, I think, to any situation of trans-lingual anthropology. Some of this has been done in Taiwan, but more of what happens in Taiwan seems to be a direct adoption of English terms either by borrowing or translation; as with Fei, some work better than others. The subaltern theorists of India might also provide an interesting comparison, but of course they are writing mostly in English, although it is English seasoned by the experience of a very un-English society. On balance, I would recommend Fei's work to any anthropologist from a non-metropolitan

---

[4] After all, he was not so stupid or blinded by any kind of nationalism, nor should anyone be so seduced by opposition to Eurocentrism to reject everything that comes out of Europe just because it comes out of Europe.

country wrestling with these problems, but with the important qualifier that if the interested anthropologist couldn't read Chinese (which would almost always be the case), it would be hard to see 90% of the model that he or she was seeking. Since Chinese is not a language of metropolitan discourse[5], what might have been an important prospective model for the internationalization of theory is probably consigned to obscurity. Once it is translated, however valuable its analysis, its value as a model disappears behind a thick screen.

Second, we should consider the value of *Xiangtu Zhongguo* for China's current attempt to revive and indigenize anthropology. Ironically and rather sadly, the promise and the model of *Xiangtu Zhongguo* did not survive in Fei-after-Mao, in the roly-poly octo- and then nonagenarian who emerged from political disgrace and defended Malinowski and Mao in the same breath. The only thing he could say in his 1984 preface to the Sanlian edition of *Xiangtu Zhongguo* was that it might be fun after forty years to see his own youthful musings in print again (1985: III). Obviously, Fei might have been prouder of his own achievement than this politically cautious modesty would indicate, but he was also intelligent enough that he could have hinted at greater significance for the present, had he chosen to. Instead he extolled the model of Malinowski. Perhaps this is because he really wanted to encourage a return to more empirical work and avoid so much empty theorizing, and not because he really believed in seventy-year-old functionalism. Whatever the case, he was not the one to express or advocate the significance of his own work. This will have to come directly from the younger generations, unscarred by the mindless orthodoxy of revolutionary Marxist ethnology, whose works will be represented in the next issue of this journal.

Finally, perhaps the greatest significance for us as anthropologists is to alert us to the significance of particular languages, to the far from frictionless nature of the translation process, even in so technical and jargon-filled a field as anthropology. Having read *Xiangtu Zhongguo,* we can never again consider translation of scholarly work from one language to another to be un-problematical; rather the problematic of translation, not only of field data but also of the scholarly product, must remain central to our understanding of the intellectual and political future of our discipline.

References

Asad, Talal. 1973. *Anthropology and the Colonial Encounter.* London: Ithaca Press.
Benedict, Ruth. 1946. *The Chrysanthemum and the Sword: Patterns of Japanese Culture.* Boston: Houghton, Mifflin.
Bott, Elizabeth. 1971[1957]. *Family and Social Network: Roles Norms, and External Relationships in Ordinary Urban Families.* London: Tavistock Publications.
Cai Yuanpei. 1962[1926]. *On Ethnology.* In Cai Yuanpei, Reprinted. *Minzuxue Lunshu,* Taipei: Zhonghua Shuju. (蔡元培:说民族学 《民族学论述》，台北：中华书局1962年重印).

---

[5] And despite the proliferation of Confucius Institutes is likely never to become one, given its writing system.

Fei, Hsiao-t'ung (Fei Xiaotong 费孝通). 1939. *Peasant Life in China: A Field Study of Country Life in the Yangtze Valley.* New York: E.P. Dutton.

— 1985[1947]. *Xiangtu Zhongguo* (in Chinese), Beijing: SDX Joint Publishing Company. (费孝通: 《乡土中国》, 北京: 三联书店,1985年重印).

— 1992. *From the Soil: The Foundations of Chinese Society.* Translation of Fei Xiaotong's *Xiangtu Zhongguo* with an introduction and epilogue by Gary Hamilton and Wang Zheng, Berkeley and Los Angeles: University of California Press.

Freedman, Maurice. 1958. *Lineage Organization in Southeastern China.* London: Athlone Press.

— 1966. *Chinese Lineage and Society.* New York: Humanities Press.

Harrell, Stevan. 2001. *Ways of Being Ethnic in Southwest China.* Seattle and London: University of Washington Press.

— 2002. Another Discussion of *minzu* and *zuqun*: Reply to Professor Li Shaoming, *MinzuYanjiu* (Nationalities Studies, Beijing), 2002, 6: 36-40. (郝瑞: 再谈"民族"与"族群"—回应李绍明教授.《民族研究》2002年第6期).

Harrell, Stevan, and Li Xingxing. 2011. *Wenben Shamo, Qinggan Lüzhou* (Textual Desert, Emotional Oasis), *Renleixue Pinglun* (*Anthropological Critique*), Beijing (郝瑞、李星星: 文本沙漠, 情感绿洲, 《人类学评论》, 2011年).

Hu, Hsien-chin. 1948. *The Common Descent Group in China and its Functions.* New York: Viking Fund.

Kenyatta, Jomo. 1938. *Facing Mount Kenya: The Tribal Life of the Gikuyu.* London: Secker and Warburg.

Knight, Nick. 1990. Soviet Philosophy and Mao Zedong's 'Sinification of Marxism'. *Journal of Contemporary Asia.* 20 (1). pp. 89-109.

Lévi-Strauss, Claude. 1962. *Le totemisme aujourd'hui.* Paris: Presses universitaires de France.

Lin Yueh-hwa (Lin Yaohua). 1948. *The Golden Wing: A Sociological Study of Chinese Familism.* London: Kegan Paul, Trench and Trubner.

Radcliffe-Brown, A.R. 1929. Notes on Totemism in Eastern Australia. *Journal of the Royal Anthropological Institute of Great Britain and Ireland* 59. pp. 399-415.

Rivers, W.H.R. 1909. Totemism in Polynesia and Melanesia. *Journal of the Royal Anthropological Institute of Great Britain and Ireland* 39. pp. 156-180.

Said, Edward W. 1978. *Orientalism.* New York: Pantheon Books.

Schulte, Rainer and Biguenet, John. 1992. *Theories of Translation: An Anthology of Essays from Dryden to Derrida.* Chicago: University of Chicago Press.

Steiner, George. 1975. *After Babel: Aspects of Language and Translation.* New York: Oxford University Press.

Williams, Raymond. 1973. *The Country and the City.* New York: Oxford University Press.

Wylie, Raymond F. 1979. Mao Tse-tung, Ch'en Po-ta and the 'Sinification of Marxism,' 1936-38. *The China Quarterly* 79. pp. 447-80.

DOI https://doi.org/10.24103/GCSS1.en.2015.4

Moulüe (Supraplanning)
On the problem of the transfer of earthbound words and concepts in the context of cultural exchange between China and the West

Harro von Senger

Abstract: According to Fei Xiaotong, 'Words are the most important bridge' (词是最主要的桥梁) between past and present and between generations belonging to the same culture. They are also the most important bridge between humans belonging to different cultures. The question arises to what extend can earthbound words (that is to say words which do not seem to have a readymade exact counterpart in the foreign language concerned) be transferred from one culture to the other in such a way that they are understood and maybe even of practical use in the other cultural environment while keeping their earthboundness, that is to say their original touch and meaning. This problem is discussed with respect to the Chinese word '*moulüe* (谋略)', deeply rooted in the rich vocabulary of the ancient and modern Chinese Art of Planning.

Keywords: Intercultural communicability of earthbound words; strategy, '*moulüe* (谋略) – Supraplanning', *Sun Zi's Art of War*.[1]

According to a report entitled 'Wu Jiang commemorates Fei Xiaotong's 100th birthday' (*People's Daily* Overseas Edition, 25th October, 2010):

> after the death of Fei Xiaotong, not only the number of visitors coming to the Kaixiangong Village did not decrease, but the scope of visitors broadened to people beyond the sociological circle.[2]

This shows that Fei Xiaotong does not only attract the interest of sociologists. His appeal is much wider. As a sinologist, I can find in Fei Xiaotong's writings many valuable statements with relevance for sinology as the science of the Chinese culture based primarily on the research of material in written or spoken Chinese language. Many of Fei Xiaotong's insights can promote mutual Sino-European cultural awareness and serve as a theoretical base for the transfer of Chinese con-

---

[1] The alleged author of the Sun Zi's *Art of War* (《孙子兵法》) was originally spelt as Sun Tzu. This article uses Sun Zi based on the Chinese pinyin system. The book has commonly been referred to in three different ways: *Sun Tzu's Art of War*, *Sun Zi's Art of War*, and simply *The Art of War*

[2] 费孝通逝世后，来开弦弓村的访问者不但没有减少，而且突破了社会学界的范围.

cepts to the West.[3] The purpose of this paper is to show the importance of some of Fei Xiaotong's thoughts for sinology.

In his outstanding book *Xiangtu Zhongguo* (《乡土中国》), Fei Xiaotong says that humans, thanks to their ability to remember,

> not only bridge their own past and present, but also… generations (Fei, 1992:55; Fei 1985:17).[4]

In the Chinese text, Fei Xiaotong points out that words are the most important bridge (Fei, 1985:17).

In the English edition of *Xiangtu Zhongguo* (*From the Soil*), this phrase has been translated as '[T]his connection rests upon the ability to use words' (Fei, 1992:55). Both the original Chinese version and the English translation give me the opportunity to add a further dimension to the statement of Fei Xiaotong, namely the transcultural one. Words are not only a bridge between past and present and between generations belonging to the same culture, but also between humans belonging to different cultures. My contribution is focused on Sino-Western communication. Speaking about intercultural exchange of words and the concepts transported by those words, I always have Sino-Western exchange in mind.

The question which arises is the following: can earthbound words and concepts be transferred from one culture to the other in such a way that they are understood and maybe even of practical use in the other cultural environment while keeping their earthboundness, that is to say their original touch and meaning?

What are 'earthbound words'? With this term, I refer to words which do not seem to have a readymade exact counterpart in the foreign language. A danger arises that we choose a convenient way by translating such words using some preexisting seemingly corresponding foreign words.

Let me illustrate this problem with the Chinese word *moulüe* (谋略), a word deeply rooted in the rich vocabulary of the ancient and modern Chinese Art of Planning. It is a word with which Chinese people are very familiar, 'but which is very mysterious (Chai, 1994: 1).[5] Recently, innumerable books have been published in the People's Republic of China (PRC) on *moulüe*. Just a few examples:

- Chai Yuqiu (1991), *Moulüe Ku* (The Store of *Moulüe*), 4th edition, Beijing (柴宇球:《谋略库》).
- Chai Yuqiu (1991), *Moulüe Lun* (On *Moulüe*), Beijing (柴宇球:《谋略论》).

---

[3] The starting point was a quotation from Fei Xiaotong in von Senger (1995).

[4] 词是最主要的桥梁. Thanks to Dr Xiangqun Chang, the organizer of the conference to commemorate the centenary of Professor Fei Xiaotong's birth, for providing me both the Chinese and English versions of Fei's work.

[5] 谋略，是人们十分熟悉而又非常神秘的字眼.

- Xiao Shimei (2005), *Mao Zedong Moulüexue* (Mao Zedong's *Moulüe* Erudition), Beijing (萧诗美:《毛泽东谋略学》).
- He Kaiyao (2004), *Xiaoping Moulüe* ([Deng] Xiaoping's *Moulüe*), Beijing (贺开耀:《小平谋略》).
- Yang Qingwang (ed.) (1992), *Shiyong Moulüexue Cidian* (Practical Dictionary of the Science of *Moulüe*), Harbin (杨庆旺主编:《实用谋略学词典》).

However, as far as the 'mysterious' Chinese word *moulüe* is concerned, those Chinese authors who try to render *moulüe* into the English language simply use terms such as 'strategy' or 'stratagem'. Here two examples:

1) Gan Sheng (ed.) (1992), *Shangzhan Moulüe Anli Quan Jian*, Ürümuqi (甘生主编:《商战谋略案例全鉴》). This book title is translated on the book cover of the Chinese edition as 'The Encyclopaedia of Marketing Warfare Strategy Case'. That is to say, '*shangzhan moulüe* 商战谋略' is translated with 'warfare strategy'.

2) Li Bingyan (2004), *Da Moulüe Yu Xin Junshi Biange*, Beijing (李炳彦,《大谋略与新军事变革》). The title of this book is translated on page 390 as *Military Stratagem and the New Revolution in Military Affairs*. In other words, *moulüe* has been translated as 'stratagem'.

In the West, the Chinese term *moulüe* has until now received little academic attention. In the United States, only very few translations of *moulüe* have been published (Detweiler, 2010:9, 13-15):

1) The United States Department of Defense reported in its *Annual Report to Congress: Military Power of the People's Republic of China 2006*:

    'In recent decades there has been a resurgence in the study of ancient Chinese statecraft within the PLA. Whole departments of military academies teach *moulüe*, or strategic deception, derived from Chinese experience through the millennia....'

2) Mark Stokes[6] referred to the Chinese word *moulüe* three times in his article 'The Chinese Joint Aerospace Campaign: Strategy, Doctrine, and Force Modernization'. He wrote for instance:

    'Chinese views of deterrence and coercion differ slightly from Western perspectives. Chinese authors associate deterrence and coercion with the concept of stratagem (*moulüe*; 某略 [sic], which misspelt the character '谋') the art of winning political or military contests through clever or superior strategic ploys, operational art, or tactics...'

---

[6] Mark Stokes is a Country Director for the PRC and Taiwan within the Office of the Secretary of Defense, International Security Affairs, affiliated with the Strategic Studies Institute of the United States Army War College, former assistant air attaché at the U.S. Defense Attaché Office in Beijing from 1992-1995, and author of *China's Revolution in Doctrinal Affairs* (2005), financed by the RAND Corporation and the CAN Corporation.

3) Ralph Sawyer[7], a well-known translator of ancient Chinese military trea-
tises, devoted in his book *The Tao of Deception* (2007) a small commentary to the recent *moulüe* trend in the People's Republic of China (PRC),
and writes:

> 'Beginning in the late 1980s, but especially in 1991, coincident with
> the re-emergence of the classical military writings as viable subjects
> for investigation, there was a sudden surge of interest in strategy and
> stratagems (*mou-lüeh*)' (Sawyer, 2007:329).

In the same book, he translates *moulüe* also with 'strategy' (Sawyer, 2007:435 n.
6; 437 n. 18; 440 n. 39). This is puzzling because he also translates *zhanlüe* (战略)
as 'strategy' (Sawyer, 2007:447 n. 25; 449 n. 50).

All the above-mentioned Chinese and American authors or institutions lack
attention to detail when they use expressions such as 'strategic deception', 'stratagem', 'strategy and stratagems' or 'strategy' for *moulüe*. 'Deception' as a translation for *moulüe* is too narrow. Even when *moulüe* operates with deception, it
is not necessarily always 'strategic deception', but maybe tactical or operational
deception. 'Stratagem' and 'strategy' are also inadequate translations of *moulüe*.

A 'stratagem' is
- An operation or act of generalship; usually an artifice or trick designed to
  outwit or surprise the enemy; in generalized sense: military artifice;
- An artifice or trick; a device or scheme for obtaining an advantage; in
  generalized sense: skill in devising expedience; artifice; cunning. (*Oxford
  English Dictionary*, 1933).

A 'strategy' is
- The science of art of military command as applied to the overall planning
  and conduct of large scale combat operations.
- A plan of action resulting from the practice of this science.
- The art or skill of using stratagems in politics, business, courtship, or the
  like.... See stratagem. (*American Heritage Dictionary*, 1981:1273).
- '...a careful plan or method or a clever stratagem...' (*Webster's Third
  New International Dictionary*, 1976: 2256).

According to my understanding of the vast meaning of *moulüe*, it is not limited
to planning operations based on cunning only. Therefore, 'stratagem' as a translation of *moulüe merely* grasps one aspect of *moulüe*, not its complete meaning
going far beyond the purely 'stratagemical' dimension. As far as I understand the
English word 'strategy', it means either 'careful plan' or 'stratagem', but not the
possible combination of both aspects. Therefore, 'strategy' also misrepresents the
meaning of *moulüe*, since *moulüe* can result in a careful stratagemical plan as

---

[7] Ralph Sawyer is a leading American scholar of ancient and modern Chinese warfare, having
worked extensively with major intelligence and defense agencies, as well as a Fellow of the
Canadian Centre for Military and Strategic Studies.

well as in a careful non-stratagemical plan. Apparently, the Chinese and American translators of *moulüe* quoted above do not succeed in grasping the full meaning of *moulüe*. With their translations, they do not really introduce *moulüe* into the English language in a way that preserves its earthboundness. That is to say, they do not transfer a Chinese word and the concept which it harbors into the foreign culture. Rather, they just replace a Chinese word with a superficially corresponding Western word with quite a different – in this case smaller – meaning than the Chinese counterpart. The effect is not a cultural transfer but a Westernization of a Chinese term. Its earthboundness gets lost. The preexisting Western word does not function as – to quote Fei Xiaotong – a 'bridge', but as an 'artificial limb' which creates the *illusion* of mutual understanding and does not lead to a *real* mutual understanding.

Maybe, this way of changing something which is Chinese into something which is Western has its root in the fact that the concept transferred by the Western word is not fully understood by the Western translator. Another way to explain the simple replacing of a Chinese word by a Western word which only superficially represents the idea of the Chinese word might be the assumption that all languages have an equivalent thesaurus of words. According to this assumption, for every word in the language A, there can be found an equivalent word in any language B – earthbound words and concepts do not exist because words and concepts are universal and easily interchangeable. I think that this assumption is not true. Many words have in their language some earthbound touch, and certain words even exist uniquely in one language. These kinds of words 'resist easy formulaic translation' (Ames, 1993:71).

What does *moulüe* mean? In its technical sense, it has a rather specific significance for which no indigenous Western term is suitable. There is no other way than to create a new expression in the Western language concerned. For such a case, Confucius' advice to 'rectify the names' is not sufficient. There is a need to 'create a name' so that a certain thing can be correctly denominated.

The interest in *moulüe* in the PRC is certainly connected with the 'Science of Military *Moulüe* (*Junshi Moulüexue* 军事谋略学)', which has obtained a semi-official status in the system of the Military Science of the PRC in the last few years. Therefore, my analysis of *moulüe* is based on printed or online publications on the 'Military Science of *Moulüe*', for instance:

- Li Bingyan, Sun Jing (1989), *Junshi Moulüexue* (The Science of Military 'Moulüe'), two volumes, Beijing (李炳彦, 孙兢: 《军事谋略学》)
- Luo Zhihua (1995). *Junshi Moulüe Zhi Dao* (The Way of Military Moulüe), Beijing (罗志华《军事谋略之道》)
- *Zhongguo Moulüe Kexue Wang, Junshi Moulüe Yanjiu Zhongxin* (China 'Moulüe Science' Net, Centre of Military Moulüe Research) <http://www.szbf.net>, (中国谋略科学网, 军事谋略研究中心)

In order to discuss with him about his publications on the 'Thirty-six stratagems' and other related topics, I have met the recently retired Major General Li Bingyan many times in Beijing since the middle of the 1980. Li Bingyan is considered to be the founder and leader of the People's Liberation Army's (PLA) modern military discipline called *junshi moulüexue* (the science of military *moulüe*). He was or still is a senior editor of *PLA Daily*, a council member of the Association of News Workers of the Whole Country of China, a council member of the China Research Society of *Sun Tzu's Art of War*, and the director of the Centre for the Research of Military *Moulüe* at the PLA Military Operations Research Institute. He has received multiple military awards, and was even met by Chairman Jiang Zemin in 1996 for his contributions to the development of the science of military *moulüe*.

Before introducing my proposal for the English translation of *moulüe*, I want to reproduce a schema published by leading Chinese experts of *junshi moulüexue* (Li and Sun, 1989:9).

It is not necessary to explain the whole schema. Relevant is the fact that Marxist philosophy is positioned at the top, but even this can be put aside in this context. On the second place down from the top, we find the entry 'Science of Military *Moulüe*'. Afterwards, there are three entries at the left side, from top to bottom:

- Science of Strategy
- Science of Military Campaigns (also translatable as 'Operational Science')
- Science of Tactics

The striking point in this schema is that *moulüe* is positioned above (Latin: *supra*) 'strategy'. This means *moulüe* is situated on a higher planning level than strategy. In the West, the highest planning level is the strategic planning level. I do not know a Western word designating a planning level above the strategic planning level.

Regarding *Sun Tzu's Art of War*, with its highest ideal – according to the common interpretation – to subdue the enemy without war (Jullien, 1996:63), some authors use the English term 'grand strategy' (Sawyer and Sawyer, 1994:128; Niu, 2008:253f). What does 'grand strategy' mean? Here is a short description of this concept:

> [T]he role of grand strategy – higher strategy – is to co-ordinate and direct all the resources of a nation, or band of nations, towards the attainment of the political object of the war – the goal defined by fundamental policy.
>
> Grand strategy should both calculate and develop the economic resources and man-power of nations in order to sustain the fighting services. Also the moral resources – for to foster the people's willing spirit is often as important as to possess the more concrete forms of power. Grand strategy, too, should regulate the distribution of power between the several services, and between the services

and industry. Moreover, fighting power is but one of the instruments of grand strategy – which should take account of and apply the power of financial pressure, and, not least of ethical pressure, to weaken the opponent's will....

Furthermore, while the horizon of strategy is bounded by the war, grand strategy looks beyond the war to the subsequent peace. It should not only combine the various instruments, but so regulate their use as to avoid damage to the future state of peace – for its security and prosperity (Liddell Hart, 1954:335f.).

As one can see from this quotation, 'grand strategy' does not seem to embrace 'subduing the enemy' without war. 'Grand strategy' is a strategy for waging war. Furthermore, 'grand strategy' does not seem to take notice of the use of stratagems. It is a 'stratagem blind' concept. Therefore, I think if one describes *The Art of War* with Western concepts such as 'grand strategy' or 'total strategy' (Prestat, 2006:62), one westernizes it and eliminates its earthbound Chineseness, transforming it into a Western war theory. The reasons that the essence of *The Art of War* is beyond the reach of Western Art-of-War-terminology can be shown by a close look at this key phrase:

不战而屈人之兵善之善者也

In the Chinese text, we can see very clearly and without any doubt the Chinese character *ren* (人 men), not *di* (敌 enemy). *Di* is frequently employed in *The Art of War* (Giles, 1964: 188).[8] Why does it not appear in this sentence? For a Westerner with his Western strategic or even grand strategic outlook, this is not a question worthy of consideration. For her or him, it is clear that *ren* has, of course – or as one says in Chinese: *dangran* (当然) – the meaning of *di*. 'Un-earthbounded' Chinese commentators of *The Art of War* also think in this way. Although *ren* is written rather than *di*, as far as I know, all Western and Westernized Chinese translations of this sentence deviate from the Chinese text and translate it as if it would refer to *di*. I quote here only some representative Western versions of this phrase:

- Subjugating the **enemy's** army without fighting is the true pinnacle of excellence (Sawyer and Sawyer, 1994:177).
- The highest excellence is to subdue the **enemy's** army without fighting at all (Ames, 1993:111).
- Ultimate excellence lies not in winning every battle but in defeating the **enemy** without ever fighting (Minford, 2003: 14).
- To subdue the **enemy** without fighting is the acme of skill (Griffith, 1963:77).
- Le mieux est de soumettre l'**ennemi** sans combattre (Niquet, 2006:112).
- ...der Inbegriff der Tüchtigkeit ... ist ... derjenige, der sich die Truppen des **Gegners** ohne Kampf unterwirft (Klöpsch, 2009:17).

---

[8] According to the 'Chinese concordance' in Giles (1964:188), *di* (敌) appears 12 times in the first five chapters and « passim » in the chapters VI, IX, X, XI and XIII.

A Chinese *Sun Zi Bingfa* expert[9] whom I interviewed on the 9 June 2010 in Shanghai about the relevance of the character *ren* in the quoted sentence explained it to me in this way:

> In the sentence 不战而屈人之兵善之善者也, the object of *qu* (屈) is not necessarily the army of an imminent enemy. This sentence relates also to a currently befriended or allied counterpart. However, one is aware that in a near or even far future, this counterpart could become an enemy. Therefore, one uses already now measures such as stratagems to subdue him so that in the future he cannot become a danger. At the time when the measures subduing him without war are used, he is not an 'enemy'.

Based on this explanation of the 'simple' word *ren*, I translated this sentence into German in this way:

> *Ohne einen Waffengang die Streitmacht der* Männer *der Gegenseite gefügig machen ist erst das Gute vom Guten* (von Senger, 2011:14f.). It can be translated into English as 'Without using arms to subdue the army of the **men** of the other side is the best'.

Through this translation, which is not 'enemy'-fixed and takes the word *ren* seriously, the sentence gets quite a new and much longer time dimension than in the common Western or Westernized Chinese translations. Without exception, they seem to be dominated by the relatively short-sighted Western strategic or even 'grand strategic' thinking, whereas the original Chinese sentence creates the impression of much more than that. As long as one is imprisoned in Western terminology, one remains dependent on Western thought patterns, with the result that one 'sees but does not get aware' (*shi er bu jian* 视而不见) of the word *ren* and its far-reaching meaning. This shows the importance of the awareness of the earth-boundness of one's own as well as of the Chinese world outlook.

By the way, isn't under our eyes 不战而屈人之兵善之善者也 being implemented, namely by the PRC? For many years, it has been steadily economically binding Taiwan (not considered as an 'enemy') more and more narrowly to itself, thus making Taiwanese 'independence' gradually impossible and realizing, very softly, 'on Panda paws', an unspectacular peaceful 'reunification'.

Since 'strategy' or 'grand strategy' does not fit with the extraordinarily 'long term' (Jullien, 1996:101) forecasting horizon exposed in the key quotation of traditional Chinese military thinking just discussed, that supreme excellence consists in subduing the army of the men of the other side without using arms (不战而屈人之兵善之善者也), I propose to characterize the essence of the Art of Planning described in *The Art of War* not with a preexistent Western term, but with the

---

[9] Qi Wen, the co-editor of *Sun Zi Bingfa Da Cidian* (*Great Encyclopaedia of Sun Zi Bingfa*), Shanghai 1994, *Sun Zi Bingfa Shi Jiang* (*Ten Lectures on Sun Zi Bingfa*), Shanghai 2007, and other related books (戚文:《孙子兵法大辞典》, 1994年,《孙子兵法十讲》, 2007年等).

Chinese word *moulüe*. But how should *moulüe* be translated so that it keeps its earthboundness?

Before I answer this question, I want to make a preliminary remark about the idea of transplanting the Chinese term *moulüe* untranslated, only in its transcription, into Western languages. This might be at first glance a clever way to evade the distortion caused by an inadequate translation. However, if *moulüe* is left untranslated, it remains nevertheless necessary to explain its meaning. In the end, nothing is gained. I maintain my optimism that the Western languages have the capacity to offer appropriate translations of earthbound words from foreign cultures. What matters is to really grasp the essential meaning of those words, for instance of *moulüe*.

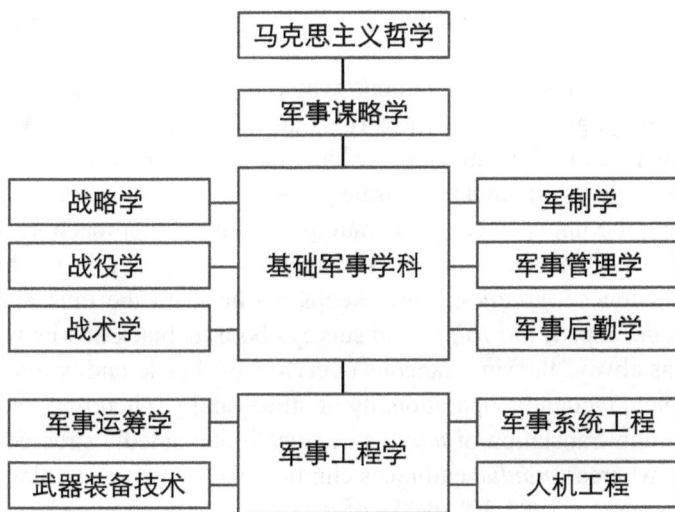

图 1-4

Figure 1 The structure of Chinese military science

Two Reasons for Translating *Moulüe* as 'Supraplanning'

Let me return to the schema taken from Li Bingyan's book on *junshi moulüexue* (see Figure 1).

The fact that *moulüe* is positioned above (Latin: *supra*) the Western strategic planning level is the first reason why I have chosen 'supraplanning' as the translation of *moulüe*. The word 'supraplanning' as seen from this schema is intended to indicate that *moulüe* has – in its extreme form – time dimensions which are far longer than the common Western strategic and even 'grand strategic' planning intervals.

The second reason for the translation 'supraplanning' is connected with another quality of *moulüe* which can be explained with the well-known *Taijitu*:

Figure 2: *Taijitu* diagram

Moulüe-planning is not just fixed in the white or in the black hemisphere of the *Taijitu*. In this context, the white sphere can be understood as designating the whole set of problem-solving methods which are based on transparency, regularity, conformity, generally accepted rules and ways of thinking. Western game theory has its place in the white sector. The black part symbolizes all those problem-solving methods which are not transparent, not conforming to routine thinking but 'doing the unexpected and pursuing the indirect approach' (Liddell Hart, 1980, p. VII). For instance, the '36 stratagems' are situated in the black hemisphere. The Chinese *moulüe*-planner keeps his head all the time above (in the Latin language: *supra*) the *Taijitu* and surveys both its black and its white sphere so that he has always the simultaneous overview of 'black' and 'white' options to solve a problem tactically, operationally or strategically. Therefore, 'stratagem' is not the optimum translation of *moulüe* because it one-sidedly stresses the 'black' hemisphere, whereas *moulüe* embraces cunning and non-cunning planning.

Li Bingyan (Li, 1983:30) speaks of

> 'a hawk of supraplanning thought' (*moulüe siwei de ying* 谋略思维的鹰) which, soaring in the sky, looks down on the concrete battlefield

and selects either 'orthodox' (*zheng* 正) or unorthodox (*qi* 奇) options to act. Sometimes both options are combined. As the black spot in the white hemisphere indicates, in an orthodox problem solution, some unorthodox, stratagemical element can be integrated. A person with not only a legal but also a supraplanning mind is aware of the fact that for instance a legal norm (orthodoxy) can harbor some stratagemical intention (unorthodoxy).

For example, Article 5 of the *Law of the People's Republic of China on Chinese-Foreign Joint Ventures* (1 July 1979, stipulates:

> Each party to a joint venture may make its investment in cash, in kind or in industrial property rights, etc. The technology and the equipment that serve as the investment of the foreign partner in a joint venture must be advanced technology and equipment that actually suit our country's needs. If the foreign partner in a joint venture causes losses by deception through the intentional use of backward technology and equipment, he shall pay compensation for these losses.

Equipped with the supraplanning approach, one gets quickly aware that in this legal norm, at least two of the 36 stratagems are involved, namely stratagem no. 19 'Removing the firewood from under the cauldron' and stratagem no. 30 'changing the role of the guest for that of the host'. The PRC uses joint ventures to extract advanced technology in a legal way from Western enterprises (stratagem no. 19) with the ultimate aim of implementing stratagem no. 30, namely changing from a country which has to rely on and to pay for foreign technology into a country with its own technology which it can sell on its own conditions or even not sell to other countries. As seen from a supraplanning perspective, one must always keep in mind, even while reading legal texts, that some stratagem could be hidden there. Supraplanning advocates thus a 'black-white' analytical mind.

The planning outlook of a *moulüe*-expert is above (Latin: *supra*) the two big alternative problem-solving mechanisms: the orthodox and the unorthodox way to achieve an objective. Therefore, *moulüe*-planning is constantly oscillating between normal and norm deviating (here not in a criminal, but legally acceptable sense) scenarios of problem resolution.

This is quite different from any Western decision-making theory which I know of. Western decision-making theories are very strongly reliant on the 'white' game theory, mathematics and so on. A systematic theory of the strategic, operational and tactical applicability of the Art of Cunning with respect to any kind of problem is, as far as I know, lacking in the West. Whereas the 'white' problem resolutions are based on intellectual efforts, stratagems are used in the West certainly very often, but mostly based not on the intellect but on pure intuition, without careful stratagemical planning.

Moulüe Practice in the People's Republic of China

President Richard Nixon said in a speech given at Peking University:

> It is said that in the United States, one is thinking in decades…but in China, one is thinking in centuries (Ying, 1988:210f.).

And Al Gore wrote in his report 'A Generational Challenge to Repower America' (July 17, 2008):

> Ten years is about the maximum time that we as a Nation can hold steady aim and hit our target (Gore, 2008).

In other words, the longest strategic planning horizons in the most important Western country are ten years.

It is quite different in the PRC. During his journey to the South in the year 1992, Deng Xiaoping coined the phrase:

> Uphold the Party's basic line, one hundred years unwavering.

According to the *Constitution10 of the Communist Party of China* (CPC), revised and adopted at the 18th National Congress of the CPC on November 14, 2012, presently (2013) in force,

> China is in the primary stage of socialism and will remain so for a long time to come. This is a historical stage which cannot be skipped in socialist modernization in China which is backward economically and culturally. **It will last for over a hundred years**.

Furthermore, in the Constitution of the CCP, there are enshrined two 100-year targets (*bai nian da ji* 百年大计 in Chinese phrase):

> The... objectives of economic and social development at this new stage in the new century are to consolidate and develop the relatively comfortable life initially attained, bring China into a moderately prosperous society of a higher level to the benefit of well over one billion people by the time of the Party's centenary [**till 2021**] and bring the per capita GDP up to the level of moderately developed countries and realize modernization in the main by the time of the centenary of the People's Republic of China [**till 2049**].

These two 100-year-targets were already enshrined in previous Constitutions, for instance that of 2002 and 2007. As early as in the middle 1980s, Hu Yaobang, Chairman of the CCP, had predicted that in order to become prosperous and strong, the PRC would have to strive for between 30 and 50 years after the turn of the century (von Senger, 1985b).

The extremely vast Chinese time horizon, being longer than the longest US planning horizons, parallels the ancient Chinese fable called 'The Foolish Old Man Who Removed the Mountains'. It tells of an old man who lived in northern China long ago and was known as the Foolish Old Man of North Mountain. His house faced south and beyond his doorway stood the two great peaks, Taihang and Wangwu, obstructing the way. He called his sons and, hoes in hand, they began to dig up these mountains with great determination. Another old man, known as the Wise Old Man, saw them and said derisively, 'How silly of you to do this! It is quite impossible for you few to dig up those two huge mountains.' The Foolish Old Man replied, 'when I die, my sons will carry on; when they die, there will be my grandsons, and then their sons and grandsons, and so on to infinity. High as they are, the mountains cannot grow any higher and with every bit we dig, they will be that much lower. Why can't we clear them away?'

---

10 Note: I oppose the word 'Constitution' with respect to the 《中国共产党章程》. A 章程 as a technical term is not a 'constitution'. I know that on the Internet, the term 'Constitution' is used with respect to the 《中国共产党章程》, but this translation has certainly not been made by a legally educated person. Non-legal persons aren't aware of the nuances of the norm-oriented terminology. 'Constitution' is correct for 《中华人民共和国宪法》. 'Constitution' as a technical term is a legal term. The Statute of the CCP does not belong to the law of the Chinese state. Therefore I prefer the technical term 'Statute'.

This wide supraplanning horizon is also reflected in sayings like that of Chen Danran (陈澹然) (1860-1930), often cited in Chinese books on *moulüe*:

> Since ancient times, those who did not 'devise plans' for ten thousand generations were not capable of devising plans for one era; those who did not devise plans for the whole situation were not capable of devising plans for one area (Li, 1983:4).[11]

What does the awareness of Chinese political supraplanning mean for instance for the Western businessman? It means many things. Here, only one aspect can be mentioned. It is the long-time horizon of the plans of the CCP. The planning horizon runs until 2021 and 2049. In this long time period, the PRC will need foreign business contacts, otherwise it cannot overcome the backwardness characterizing the 'more than 100 years' of the 'primary stage of socialism'. This generates a high degree of planning security for Western business. On the other hand, Westerners should not overlook the second aspect of 'supraplanning' and should get well acquainted with the Chinese art of cunning. Without this knowledge, they cannot match the supraplanning of their Chinese business partners.

Overcoming the Earthbound 'Encoded Eye'

In creating a new Western word, I have a good companion in Stephan Feuchtwang. He translated Fei Xiaotong's term *chaxugeju* as 'social egoism' (Hamilton and Chang, 2011:20), which is different from 'the differential mode of association' that Hamilton and Wang Zheng translated (Fei, 1992:60). The way I coined 'supraplanning', which is not a literal translation of *moulüe* but tries to grasp its sophisticated technical meaning, resembles the way the expression 'social egoism' was coined for *chaxugeju*, because 'social egoism' like 'supraplanning' is not a direct word-to-word translation, but tries to reflect the content of the word in question.

Indeed, 'supraplanning' is not the first new Western word which I have proposed for rendering a Chinese word. In another context, I formed the new German word '*Polaritätsnorm*' for the Chinese technical term *fangzhen* (方针), used by the CCP to denominate party-issued norms which regulate 'opposite' aspects of certain matters such as 'one country, two systems' or 'self-reliance as primary and striving for foreign aid as secondary'. Stuart R. Schram translated 'Polaritätsnorm' with 'duality norm' (von Senger, 1985a:171-207, esp. 177). The common English translation of *fangzhen* is 'orientation' or 'general policy', but these English words do not reveal the sophisticated structure of the Chinese Communist Party's *fangzhen*.

Sometimes, a Western word functions as an excellent 'bridge' for a Chinese word. Therefore, the necessity to invent a new Western word does not always arise, even if the Chinese word to be translated is rather earthbound. For instance,

---

[11] 自古不谋万世者,不足谋一时;不谋全局者,不足谋一域.

the Chinese word *ji* (计) in the Chinese expression *sanshiliu ji* (三十六计) can very well be rendered by the preexisting Western term 'stratagem', a word which goes back to the ancient Greek word *strategema* and has in the modern Western languages the double meaning of a ruse of war and a trick in a general sense (von Senger, 1991:1 ff.).

What is the use of having created a new Western word for the Chinese *moulüe*?

First, through the encounter with this new word, it is hoped that Westerners in general will become aware:

- that China has its own words and concepts,
- that for instance the English or the German language is sometimes too earthbound and too poor for the complexity of the world, and
- that based on the vocabulary of their earthbound languages, they do not understand all nuances of the foreign cultural heritage.

If the word 'supraplanning' shocks Westerners a little bit, because they wonder what it means and because they do not understand it without some explanation, the word will have achieved its intended effect. Westerners should be conscious of their 'encoded eye' (Foucault, 2008:12). They should know that this 'encoded eye' is the result of the fundamental codes of their culture – those governing their Western language, their Western schemas of perception, their Western values, and the hierarchy of their Western practices, which establish for every Westerner the empirical orders with which he will be dealing, and in which he will be at home. Of course, Chinese people also have their 'encoded eye'. In the intercultural exchange and mutual learning, one must be aware of the different 'encoded eyes'. This idea also seems to be one of Fei Xiaotong, who speaks about the 'focus of attention' (Fei, 1992:56). He says that 'those things having no relevance in our lives go unnoticed' (Fei, 1992:56). That seems to me to be another way of speaking about Foucault's 'encoded eye.' What, according to the Western 'encoded eye', seems to have no relevance, might in reality have relevance. The Western 'encoded eye' fits with the Western world, but probably not with the entire world, of which China is a most important part. From this point of view, Fei Xiaotong's thoughts on *Xiangtu Zhongguo* (*From the Soil*, 1992[1947]) and *Earthbound China* (Fei and Chang, 1948) have not only a significance for China but also a global significance. In the world of the 21st century, Earthbound China and Earthbound Occident should on the one hand keep their earthbound originality, but on the other mutually open themselves to each other, in an authentic and creative manner, promoting real mutual understanding; not through illusionary but rather through earthbound-related 'word bridges'. If we 'outsiders studying China' (Hamilton and Chang, 2011:22) proceed in this way, we can certainly bring an 'extra dimension' (Hamilton and Chang, 2011: 22) to our Western culture.

References

The American Heritage Dictionary of the English Language (1981) Boston: Houghton Mifflin Company.

Ames, Roger (1993) *Sun-Tzu: The Art of Warfare, the first English translation incorporating the recently discovered Yin-ch`ueh-shan texts*. Translated with an introduction and commentary. New York: Ballantine Books.

Chai, Yuqiu (ed.) (1991) Foreword, *Moulüe Ku* (The Store of 'Moulüe', 4th edition, Beijing: Lantian Publishing House) (柴宇球主编:《谋略库》, 北京: 蓝天出版社, 1991年第4版, 前言).

Detweiler, Christopher (2010) *An Introduction to the Modern Chinese Science of Military Supraplanning*. (Ph.D. thesis). University of Freiburg. Available at: <http://oatd.org/oatd/record?record=oai%5C:freidok.uni-freiburg.de-opus%5C:7726> [accessed 18 August 2013].

Fei, Xiaotong (1985[1947]) *Xiangtu Zhongguo* (in Chinese), Beijing: SDX Joint Publishing Company (费孝通:《乡土中国》, 北京: 三联书店, 1947年).

— (1992) *From the Soil: The Foundations of Chinese Society*. Translation of Fei Xiaotong's *Xiangtu Zhongguo* with an introduction and epilogue by Gary Hamilton and Wang Zheng, Berkeley: University of California Press.

Fei, Xiaotong and Chang, Tse-i. 1948. Earthbound China: A Study of Rural Economy in Yunnan. London: Routledge & Kegan Paul, 1948. (费孝通, 张之毅:《被土地束缚的中国: 云南乡村经济研究》, 伦敦, 1948年。又名: 《云南三村》, 中国社会科学文献出版社, 2006年).

Foucault, Michel (2008[1966]) *Les mots et les choses: Une archéologie des sciences humaines*. Paris: Gallimard.

— *The Order of Things: An Archaeology of the Human Sciences*. (1982[1970]) Tavistock Publications ([法]米歇尔•福柯著, 莫伟民译, 《词与物人文科学考古学》, 上海三联书店, 2002年).

Giles, Lionel (1964[1919]) *Sun Tzu on the Art of War. Translation, Introduction and Critical Notes*. Reprinted in Taipei: Literature House, Ltd. (赖安尔•瞿尔斯 (Lionel Giles 翻译和评论):《孙子兵法》, 上海/伦敦, 1919年原版; 台北 1964年再版).

Gore, Al (2008) 17 July *Speech on Climate Change*, [online] Available at: <http://www.mahalo.com/al-gore-climate-change-speech-july-17-2008> [Accessed 18 August 2013].

Griffith, Samuel (1980[1963]) *Sun Tzu: The Art of War. Translation and Introduction*, with Foreword by Basil Liddell Hart. London/Oxford/New York: Oxford University Press.

Hamilton, Gary and Chang, Xiangqun (2011) 'China and World Anthropology: A conversation on the legacy of Fei Xiaotong (1910-2005), *Anthropology Today*, No. 6.

Jullien, François (1996) *Traité de l'efficacité*. Paris: Grasset.

Klöpsch, Volker (2009) *Sunzi. Die Kunst des Krieges*: Übertragung aus dem Chinesischen und Nachwort. Frankfurt a.M. und Leipzig: Insel Verlag.

Law of the People's Republic of China on Chinese-Foreign Joint Ventures. 2001. China.org.cn. [online] Available at: < http://www.china.org.cn/ english/features/investment/36752.htm> [Accessed 16 August 2013].

Li, Bingyan (1983) *Bingjia Quanmou* (Cunning Plans of Military Experts), Beijing: Chinese People's Liberation Army Publishing House (李炳彦:《兵家权谋》, 北京: 解放军出版社, 1983年).

Li, Bingyan and Sun, Jing (1989) *Junshi Moulüexue* (Military Moulüe Science), volume 1, Beijing: Chinese People's Liberation Army Publishing House (李炳彦, 孙兢:《军事谋略学》(上下), 北京: 解放军出版社, 1989年).

Liddell Hart, Basil (1967[1954]) *Strategy*. 2nd Edn. Meridian/New York: Penguin.

— (1980[1963]) 'Foreword' in S. Griffith, *Sun Tzu: The Art of War. Translation and introduction*. London, Oxford and New York: *Oxford University Press*.

Minford, John (2003) *The Art of War. Sun-tzu (Sunzi): The essential translation of the classic book of life*. New York: Penguin.

Niquet, Valérie (2006) *Sun Zi. L'art de la guerre. Traduction et édition critique*. Paris: Economica.

Niu, Xianzhong (2008) 'Niu Xianzhong about Sun Zi Bingfa', in Sima, Qi (Ed.), *Shi Jia Lun Sun* (Ten Experts discuss Sun [Zi Bingfa]), Shanghai: Shanghai People's Publishing House. (钮先钟论孙子兵法，见司马琪 主编：《十家论孙》，上海:上海人民出版社, 2008年).

The Oxford English Dictionary (1933) Vol. 10, Oxford: Clarendon Press.

Prestat, Maurice (2006) 'Introduction' in Valérie Niquet, *Sun Zi. L'Art de la guerre. Traduction et édition critique*. Paris: Economica.

Sawyer, Ralph (2007) *The Tao of Deception: Unorthodox Warfare in Historic and Modern China*. New York: Basic Books.

Sawyer, Ralph and Sawyer, Mei-chün Lee (1994) *Sun-tzu: The Art of War. Translation, Introductions and Commentary*. Boulder: Westview Press.

von Senger, Harro (1985a) 'Recent Developments in the Relations between State and Party Norms in the People's Republic of China' in Stuart Schram (ed.), *The Scope of State Power in China*. London etc.: SOAS and The Chinese University Press.

— (1985b) 'Zukunftsziele im Reich der Mitte'. *Neue Zürcher Zeitung*, 10 April, p. 5.

— (1991) *The Book of Stratagems*, New York: Penguin.

— (1995) 'Earthbound China - Earthbound Sinology: On the Feasibility of Cultural Transfer from China to Europe'. *Archív Orientální* (63). pp. 352-359.

— (2008) *Supraplanung: Unerkannte Denkhorizonte aus dem Reich der Mitte*. München: Hanser Verlag.

— (2011) *Meister Suns Kriegskanon* translation, annotation and commentary. Stuttgart: Philipp Reclam jun.

— (2013) *Die Klaviatur der 36 Strategeme. In Gegensätzen denken lernen*, München: Hanser Verlag.

Webster's Third New International Dictionary of the English Language Unabridged (1976) Springfield: G. & C. Merriam Company.

Ye, Xiaonan (2010) Wujiang jinian Fei Xiaotong bainian danchen. *People's Daily* (Overseas Edition) 25 October. [online] Available at: < http://pap er.people.com.cn/rmrbhwb/html/2010-10/25/content_653151.htm> [Accessed 16th August 2013] (叶晓楠: 吴江纪念费孝通百年诞辰,《人民日报(海外版)》, 2010年10月25日第04 版).

Ying, Fan (Ed. and Trans.) (1988) *Waiguo Lingdaoren Fang Hua Jianghua Xuanbian* (Selected Speeches of Visiting Foreign Leaders (English-Chinese contrast). Beijing: China Translation and Publishing House. (英帆 编译:《外国领导人访华讲话选编》(英汉对照), 北京:中国对外翻译出版公司, 1988年).

Zhongguo Gongchandang Zhangcheng (Constitution of the Communist Party of China, amended and adopted at the 17th National Congress of the CPC on 21 October, 2007. [online] Available at: < http://www.Chinadaily. com.cn/language_tips/2007-10/31/content_6219108.htm>. [Accessed 16 August 2013] (《中国共产党章程》 (17大)，2007年10月21日通过，英汉对照http://news.sina.com.cn/c/2007-10-25/175914163728.shtml)

Zhongguo Gongchandang Zhangcheng (Constitution of the Communist Party of China, revised and adopted at the 18th National Congress of the CPC on 14 November, 2012. [online] Available at: < http://www.china.org.cn/ chinese/18da/2012-11/19/content_27156212.htm >. [Accessed 16 August 2013] (《中国共产党章程》(18大)，2012年11月14日通过，汉英对照.).

DOI https://doi.org/10.24103/GCSS1.en.2015.5

What Western Social Scientists Can Learn from the Writings of Fei Xiaotong[1]

Gary G. Hamilton

Abstract: This article elaborates on Fei's contrast between Chinese and Western societies that lies at the core of his book, *Xiangtu Zhongguo* (《乡土中国》). I further develop this contrast to show its relevance to sociological theories of Western and Chinese societies. This task is important not only for Western scholars, who can learn from Fei's analysis, but also for Chinese scholars, who misinterpret Fei's analysis of Chinese society because they concentrate only on the Chinese half of Fei's comparison between Chinese and Western societies and thus fail to understand the theoretical depth of his work. This article conceptualizes Fei's contrasts in order to correct Weber's flawed analysis of Chinese society.

Keywords: Fei Xiaotong, Max Weber, domination, legitimacy, *xiao* (孝), *chaxugeju* (差序格局), *tuantigeju* (团体格局)

Fei Xiaotong (or Fei Hsiao-Tung 1910–2005) was China's foremost social scientist in the 20th century. Scholars working on Chinese societies regard Fei's work as being one of the most important contributions toward building a Sinocentric, grounded sociology of Chinese society. As we celebrate the centennial anniversary of his birth, one of the questions I think we should ask is why his writings are not better known in the United States and Europe. Perhaps the answer is obvious. Because Fei's work is mostly written in Chinese and is largely about Chinese society, his ideas have not travelled well. Certainly this is part of the answer, but writing in a foreign language about a foreign place has not stopped Foucault or Habermas or Bourdieu from developing wide readerships in the U.S. I think the answer is more complex than this, and, as I will explain, I think it has to do with the style and content of Fei's work, both of which mask the groundbreaking aspects of his theoretical writings. Without a doubt, Fei's work deserves to be better known by Western readers, not only because of Fei's deep insights into the nature of Chinese society, but also because his ideal–typical contrast between Chinese and Western societies points the way to a new understanding of Western society.

In this paper, I want to elaborate on Fei's comparison between Chinese and Western societies that lies at the core of his book, *Xiangtu Zhongguo* (《乡土中

---

[1] The paper has been written for 'Understanding China and Engaging with Chinese People – The 100th Anniversary of the Birth of Professor Fei Xiaotong', an international conference commemorating the birth of Professor Fei Xiaotong, held at the London School of Economics, December 5, 2010.

国》). In Wang Zheng and my English translation of this book, published under the title *From the Soil: The Foundations of Chinese Society* (1992), I have called this comparison a contrast between an 'organizational mode of association (*tuantigeju*团体格局)' and a 'differential mode of association (*chaxugeju*差序格局).' My presentation will further develop this distinction and show its relevance to sociological theories of Western and Chinese society. This task is important not only for Western scholars, who can learn from Fei's analysis, but also for Chinese scholars, who misinterpret Fei's analysis of Chinese society because they concentrate only on the Chinese half of Fei's comparison between Chinese and Western societies and thus fail to understand the theoretical depth of his work.

Some Background

Before I start this discussion, let me very briefly provide the context that moved Fei to write *Xiangtu Zhongguo* in the first place. Fei wrote this book in the years immediately after World War II and published it, chapter by chapter, in *Shiji pinglun* (《世纪评论》), a journal widely read by intellectuals, in the years leading up to the Chinese revolution in 1949. Fei's purpose in writing this book, and also its companion volume, *Xiangtu chongjian* (*Reconstructing Rural China* 《乡土重建》), was to inform his Chinese readers that Chinese society rested on very different institutional foundations from those of Western societies and that those who wanted to reform China needed to recognize these differences and build on them.

Xiangtu Zhongguo is disarming. It is short and with few scholarly pretensions. The themes are simply, if elegantly, presented. Without knowing a lot about the themes of the book, there is no way that readers could recognize the depth of Fei's understanding of either Chinese or Western society. Most of the famous European social scientists who develop wide readerships in the U.S. announce their profundity, and through passages of difficult prose they force their readers to figure them out. But Fei hides his wisdom, remains modest in his ambitions, and gently persuades his readers to follow him on what seems like an anecdotal journey through Chinese society. The Chinese readers are left with the impression that there is no real theory here, just a series of telling observations about the way rural China works, or is it the way traditional Chinese society works, or is it the way China at the time of Fei's writing works? The reader is never actually clear what China Fei is writing about, and this ambiguity is, I believe, a part of Fei's design. He is trying to get his well-educated and somewhat aloof urban Chinese readers to recognize that they, too, think and act like Chinese everywhere. They, too, come 'from the soil.'

Fei's Use of Two Simple Analogies

Xiangtu Zhongguo is Fei's most theoretical work, and yet the theory in this book remains so hidden from most readers that they do not recognize the significance of Fei's attempt to develop a sociology of Chinese society. The core contrast on which the book is based is not even introduced until the fourth chapter, but then in every subsequent chapter, Fei goes from one institutional sphere to another to deepen this contrast. In short, pithy chapters, he covers interpersonal relations, kinship, gender relations, legitimate domination, structures of authority, social and geographical mobility, and finally what we might call a phenomenology of everyday life. But Fei's analysis is so brief and without the traditional signposts of scholarship that it is difficult to follow the theoretical progression of his ideas. As a consequence, the chapters seem more disjointed than they actually are, which is probably a consequence of its serial publication.

What most readers come away with are the two analogies, the rock-in-the-pond and the haystack analogies, that represent, respectively, Chinese and Western society. This contrast between Chinese and Western societies, which lies at the heart of the book, is carried by these two analogies. It all seems so simple, and even insignificant. However, when I first read *Xiangtu Zhongguo* in 1984, I happened to be working on a very similar problem. I was trying to understand and describe the differences between *xiao* and *patria potestas,* which is a comparison that a number of Western writers used to show the similarity between traditional Chinese and Roman societies.[2] The most notable person to use this comparison was Max Weber, the famous German social scientist who is often regarded as one of the three founders of the discipline of sociology. As I will explain in detail below, Weber linked *xiao*, usually translated as filial piety, with *patria potestas*, which in Roman law defines the patriarch's power within his household. I had already understood that Weber had made a serious typological error when he equated the two (Hamilton, 1985), but as I read *Xiangtu Zhongguo*, I immediately recognized that here was a new way, an insider Chinese way, to articulate the differences. I also knew then that, because no one else had translated the book, I needed to do it myself. I needed to do it because I intuitively understood the theoretical problem that Fei was trying to work on, and I recognized the importance of his contribution.

The Sociological Significance of Fei's Two Analogies

In *Xiangtu Zhongguo*, Fei is trying to tell his Chinese readers in 1947 that their society is quite different from Western societies and that these differences are not superficial, but rather are profound and go to the core meaning patterns of the two societies, to what German sociologists call *Weltanschauungen*, or what we call in English 'a world view.' Fei coins a term in Chinese to describe the Chinese world view, which is an ideal–typical depiction of the organizational framework of Chinese society: *chaxugeju*. I translated this term as 'the differential mode of association,' meaning that, in normative terms, Chinese view their society as being

---

[2] See Hamilton (1984) for a discussion of other writers using the two concepts to equate Chinese and ancient Western societies.

patterned through nonequivalent, ranked categories of dyadic social relationships. To illustrate this term, Fei used an analogy of ripples radiating out from where a rock landed in a pond of water. Close to the center the ripples are larger than they are further and further from the point of impact.

The ripples signify social relationships, and everyone is at the center of his or her own specific network of social relationships.[3] The relationships closest to you are those within the family: father, mother, brothers, and sisters. Depending on your own role, you have an obligation to obey those superior to you according to their role. Each dyadic role relationship is different and suggests differences in the actions that signify one's obedience. As you move further from the core family relationships – to neighbors, classmates, fellow regionals, colleagues at work – you have yet different sets of obligations for each of those roles. For subordinates, obedience for the close relationships is normative and hence, in principle, obligatory, but for relationships further away, one, in theory, has a choice whether to comply or not. The result is an ego-centered network of social relationships of family and friends that connects everyone in a web of mutual obligations. This, Fei says, is the social world that the Chinese see and through which they have to navigate the course of their lives.

Fei sets *chaxugeju*, the differential mode of association, in opposition to a Western world view, which he called *tuantigeju*, which I translated as the 'organizational mode of association.' For this Western mode of association, he says that Western societies are like straws being collected to form a haystack. Each straw is distinct but equivalent. These straws are gathered together to form bundles, these bundles form larger bundles, and all the bundles are put together to make a haystack. With this analogy, Fei is trying to show that in the West all individuals are distinct and formally equal; they belong to organizations that have clearly defined boundaries and from which individuals obtain a sense of themselves in respect of their rights and duties. Organizations, such as a club or an office, fit into larger organizations, such as a city or a corporation, which in turn fit into larger units, such as a state or province, and so on and so forth all the way up to the all-encompassing unit, which Fei identifies as the nation state. At each level of organization, individuals are constrained to act in a certain way, with rights and duties that are fitting for that level, but otherwise they remain free to do what they wish as long as they are not infringing other people's rights and duties.

Although he might have used different analogies, Fei's selection of these motifs was not an accident. The images portrayed by these analogies are, in fact,

---

[3] In the paper in this volume, Yan (forthcoming) notes in footnote 2 that in one crucial passage, Fei used the masculine form of '*ta* (他)', but in our translation I added 'her' to make the passage 'his or her.' I used 'his or her' not to be politically correct, but to be theoretically accurate, because the point Fei is making applies equally to men and women. Had Fei been writing in English in 1947, he would have also used 'he' to refer to both men and women, and I believe that is the case here as well.

commonly and repeatedly used within the respective societies. I am not going to catalog their occurrence, but will just indicate that the images mean something in these societies, and that Fei is trying to get at these meanings.

The circle within a circle within a circle is a recurring motif in Chinese society. Take for example the carved ivory ball within a ball within a ball. This type of carving has a philosophical meaning; it depicts the Chinese world order, the innermost sphere is the family and the outermost is *tianxia* (天下), all under heaven. This meaning is yet clearer in early Chinese maps. Figure 1 shows a Chinese map from the 15th century, *Zhongguo* (中国) is depicted at the center and other countries surround it, some closer and some further away. This is map of the known world from the Chinese point of view and it shows what we now call 'China's tributary system,' a circle within a circle within a circle. There is no way that you could use this map as a guide to navigate from one country to another, but you can use this map to see relationships between countries. Some countries, like Korea, are close, while others are much further away.

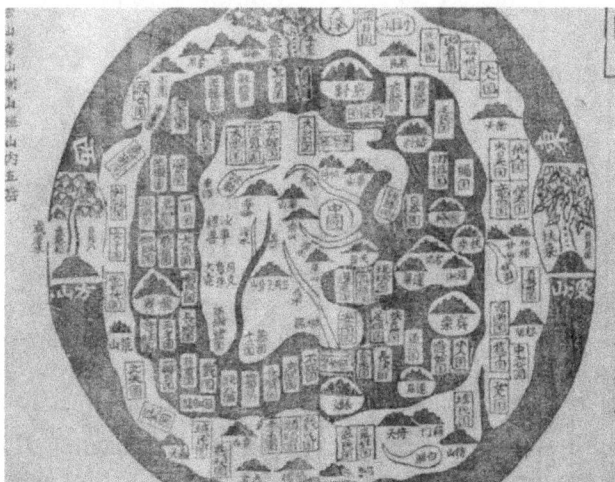

Figure 1: Fifteenth-century Chinese Map showing China's Tributary Relationships

Examples are also found in everyday life. A colleague and I recently published a paper (Hamilton & Kao, 2009), entitled 'The Round Table,' in which we argued that Taiwanese business people literally and figuratively use the idea of the round table to organize their business dealings. Most Taiwanese firms are family-owned. The owner, the *laoban* (老板), and his wife, the *laobanniang* (老板娘), form the inner core; the next group is the firm's inner circle, the *bandi* (班底), composed of a small group of employees personally loyal to the *laoban*. The *bandi* may or may not include the owner's sons. Then comes the wider group of employees who work for the firm and are treated like members of the larger family. And in the outer circles are all the other firms with whom they work in satellite assembly systems, or *weixing gongchang* (卫星工厂). Throughout the year, sitting at a round table, the *laoban* and the *laobanniang* eat lunch, almost on a daily basis, with their close employees. Sometimes for special occasions, they will host all the employees who work for them. Then at the year end, when firms host the annual *Weiya* banquet (尾牙宴), the structure of the circle, within a circle, within a circle is physically recreated with the arrangement of the round tables for the banquet. The *Weiya* banquet includes not only the *bandi* and the employees, but also the subcontractors and their employees. Everyone is placed in reference to a subtle combination of hierarchy and horizontal distance, as Yan Yunxiang (forthcoming) notes in this volume, and as I will discuss below.

Figure 2: Raphael's Disputation over the Sacrament

Now let's look at the Western image that Fei used, the straw that fits into a bundle that fits into a bale that forms a haystack. This image in Western society is ubiquitous. It is easily recognized as a simple line-and-block chart that is used to depict the authority structure of all kinds of modern organization. But even earlier, before modern organizations of this kind were common, the same organizational imagery was commonplace. Figure 2 shows the implicit meaning behind this imagery. This is a fresco painted by Raphael, called in short form the '*Disputa*,' which can be found in the Pope's private study in the Vatican. It was painted at the same time that Michelangelo painted the Sistine Chapel, in 1509. Here we see a portrait of the hierarchy of Christendom in the early 16th century. Here is God at the top holding the round earth in one hand, surrounded by the heavenly host. God looks out at us, commanding the world. Jesus is centered at the second level, flanked by the Virgin Mary and John the Baptist and joined by the prophets and the disciplines. On the ground floor are the popes, kings, cardinals, bishops, and other earthly authorities. The object of their disputation is the meaning of the sacrament.

In this fresco, just as in an ordinary line-and-block chart, everyone in the organization is subject to the authority of the person (or God) who has the upper-most position and whose power transcends the organization itself.[4] The authority of the person (or deity) in the chart not only radiates outwards but more impor-tantly is channeled into an explicit structure so that subordinates are delegated authority over some aspect of the overall organization, and each descending unit has specific rights and responsibilities relative to the overall organization. These lines of authority identify the persons having legitimate authority (i.e., the right) to command other people within that unit (or block) to fulfill the responsibilities of that unit.

Reconceptualizing Fei's Two Analogies

Let's now reconceptualize these images in a more sociological fashion. For both the Chinese and the Western sets of images, we should recognize that Fei is trying to depict a world view, but as Yan points out (Yan, forthcoming), many of Fei's critics seem to misunderstand the breadth and depth of Fei's work and to view the main concept, *chaxugeju*, as merely depicting horizontal networks of social relationships. As Fei makes very clear from chapter four on in *Xiangtu Zhongguo*, *chaxugeju* and *tuantigeju* refer to a **fundamental** ordering of, respectively, Chi-nese and Western society.

The first point to make about Fei's contrast is that these are ideal types. In the introduction to our translation of *Xiangtu Zhonggu* (Hamilton & Wang, 1992), I discuss the logic of Fei's methodology and how closely it follows the logic of ideal types first developed by Max Weber. Fei says the following in the foreword to the 1986 (pp. ii–iii) reissue of *Xiangtu Zhongguo*:

> My attempt to abstract concepts from concrete phenomena in order to under-stand the phenomena better is similar to the use of what are called ideal types in English. Ideals types belong to the realm of reason. They are neither fictitious nor ideal; rather, they are concepts formed as part of a cognitive process and are used to synthesize something that is general, so that it can be applied to concrete situations. Since a concept is formed through abstracting from concrete situa-tions, it has to be continuously tested in concrete situations in order to reduce error.

It is clear, therefore, that *chaxugeju* and *tuantigeju* are not polar opposites. In fact, they are completely unrelated; each is drawn from an analysis of the respective society; each is an attempt logically to synthesize a general aspect of that society in order, then, to analyze it in more concrete terms. These concepts are the begin-ning and not the final product of analysis, and the test of an ideal type is whether or not it is useful for that concrete analysis.

---

[4] For an extended discussion of the fresco and its meaning in the Western context, see Hamilton, 2006: Chapter One.

The second point to make is that both ideal types are constructed from the same point of view; each ideal type presents a normative view that locates the self in society. I want to emphasize 'normative.' From the point of view of the self in society, in both Chinese and Western societies, the individual person looks out on an organizational landscape that is simply taken for granted, and like fish in water, the person knows of no existence other than its watery world. This landscape is normative in the sense that this is the organizational framework of life as it **ought** to be lived and shows to individuals how they **ought** to feel, whether or not they actually live or feel this way at any particular moment.

This normative framework is a sociological landscape in four major ways. First, as children grow up in their society, they are continually socialized to recognize both the authenticity and legitimacy of this organizational framework, and to learn how to navigate their social world. Second, throughout their lives, each person must continually decide how to maneuver through their social landscape in order to take advantage of opportunities. The organizational landscape is filled with 'dos' and 'don'ts' so that a person can mentally map out how they might proceed through their world to achieve their goals. Third, this organizational landscape is consensual, is known to everyone else in society, and is constantly used as a framework to interpret the actions of others (as well as oneself). We constantly judge others by how well their other people's actions match the normative framework within which they live. Fourth, and most important, no one ever lives up to the normative ideals of their society. In fact, social rules constantly conflict with other social rules. Family and work rules often contradict, and even within families, obedience to one role may contradict obedience to another. The normative social landscape is filled with overlaps and contradictions, so that everyone violates the social rules of their society in one form or another a great deal of the time. Moreover, everyone knows that is it impossible to follow all the social rules all the time, and as a consequence there is a social vocabulary of excuses that develops in each society to account for the reasons that a person is unable to fulfill his or her obligations that arise from their position in a social landscape.

What is so insightful about Fei's ideal types is that they show, at a normative level, how differently the self is located in Chinese and Western societies. Both *chaxugeju* and *tuantigeju* contain hierarchical and horizontal components, but the contrast between the two implies a very distinct social order in each society, an order that is radically different in the two societies. That is what Fei was trying to get at. Chinese and Western societies are in the end so different because the organizational frameworks within which people create their sociological existence are configured in a very different ways.

Xiangtu Zhongguo is Fei's chief theoretical statement, and this work contains the great insight into the distinctive nature of each society and how they differ from each other. For many reasons, Fei was unable to develop this contrast in later work. But that does not mean that we, as sociologists writing over 60 years after Fei wrote this book, should not extend the exciting theoretical work that Fei began. I believe one of the best ways to extend Fei's work, as well as to make it better known in the West, is to use Fei's ideal types to correct Max Weber's misinterpretation of China.

Using Fei's Theory to Correct Weber's Analysis of China

Writing in the first two decades of the 20th century, Max Weber's great project that went through all of his writings was to scientifically explain the reasons that Western societies developed so dramatically in the 19th and early 20th centuries, while the rest of the world languished in traditional ways of life. The main, but by no means the only, mode of development was profit-oriented capitalism. To solve this historical problem, Weber developed an ideal–typical approach that centered on ideal types created from Western historical experience. As I have argued elsewhere (Hamilton, 1984, 1989), this approach led Weber to develop Eurocentric concepts. The clearest example of Weber's Eurocentric approach is found in his analysis of China. In the early version of *Economy and Society*, as well as in his first foray into comparative civilization in his analysis of China, Weber argued that patriarchalism in China was same phenomenon, typologically, as patriarchalism in the Mediterranean basin during Antiquity. In addition, Weber believed that, empirically, Chinese patriarchalism represented an even more extreme version than that which was encountered in the Western Antiquity (1951: 243). He further argued that, unlike in the West, where Christianity, especially after the Protestant Reformation, was a transformative force, religions in China were unable to break 'the fetters of the sib' (1951: 237). Confucianism and Taoism allowed for no release from patriarchy and no transformative path into rationalism and capitalism.

The core of Weber's argument equating patriarchy in Mediterranean societies with patriarchy in China centers on Weber's comparison of *patria potestas* and *xiao*. As demonstrated by his dissertation on Roman law and his later book, *The Agrarian Sociology of Ancient Civilization* (1976), Weber was a specialist on Roman law in particular and on Mediterranean cultures in Antiquity more generally. He had thought deeply about the patterns of authority throughout the Mediterranean basin and recognized that various combinations of patriarchalism and patrimonialism (i.e., the extension of the logic of patriarchalism beyond the household into the political and economic spheres) were the prevailing forms of authority throughout the region. In Roman society, however, Weber (1976: 274–292) thought patriarchalism reached its highest expression, where it was codified most thoroughly in law through the doctrine of *patria potestas*. Roman law recognized three aspects of patriarchal authority: *potestas*, the power of the head of household over his successors (i.e., his children and his children's children); *manus,* the power of the head of household over his wives and his children's wives; and *dominium*, the power of the head of household over the household's property, including slaves. In Roman law, the doctrine of *patria potestas* made the household a defined jurisdiction separate from the state, and made the head of household, the *paterfamilias*, the only person within that jurisdiction who could legitimately exercise his will.

In the last decade of his life, Weber adds a comparative dimension to his analysis of the West in order to isolate the unique civilizational features that allowed the West to develop as it did. The first comparative case Weber takes on is China, a civilization far removed from Weber's European expertise. Immersing himself in the secondary literature on China that was available to him at the time, Weber reaches the conclusion that *xiao,* which is commonly translated as filial piety, is the Chinese equivalent of *patria potestas.*[5]

> The *patria potestas,* which the head of a Roman Family retained until the end of his life, had economic and social as well as political and religious roots (the preservation of a patrician household, military affiliation according to kinship and, probably house, and the father's position as house priest). The *patria potestas* persisted during the most diverse economic stages before it was finally attenuated under the Empire, even toward the children. *In China, the same situation was perpetuated by the principle of filial piety, which was carried to an extreme by the code of duties and furthered by the state and the bureaucratic status ethic of Confucianism,* in part for reasons of political domestication (Weber, 1978: 377, my emphasis).

Weber discusses the two concepts in a number of locations in his work, and each time concludes not only that *xiao* is equivalent to *patria potestas* as a legitimating principle, but also that Chinese patriarchy is equivalent to Western patriarchy in Antiquity as an empirical configuration. The problem with this characterization is that it is inaccurate. With the help of Fei's two ideal types, we can reveal the logical structure of *patria potestas* and *xiao* and show that they are not equivalent concepts, either in typological terms or in empirical configurations to which the two relate historically.

On the one hand, *patria potestas* is emblematic of a legitimating principle that empowers people to act within the bounds of their own jurisdiction. This principle is the same as Fei conceptualized in *tuantigeju.* On the other hand, *xiao* identifies a doctrine that obliges people to submit to the duties of their own roles. This principle is the same as Fei conceptualized in *chaxugeju.* The former stresses the power and the latter the obedience of person in a position. At first glance, the two concepts look like two sides of the same coin; the power of one suggests the duty of another. This, of course, was Weber's conclusion. But, with Fei's help, we can show that they each identify quite different phenomena.

---

[5] This passage is from Weber's last draft of *Economy and Society* (1978). He also reached a similar conclusion in his work on Confucianism and Taoism (1951), which was written at least five years earlier than the passage that appears here. See Schluchter's work (1989) to date the various versions of Weber's compendium.

Toward a Theory of Chinese and Western Systems of Domination as Legitimate Jurisdictions

In theoretical terms, the two concepts differ in the characterization of both the person and the position. As a legitimating principle, *patria potestas* defines a jurisdiction and identifies the agent in that jurisdiction as the one who has the right to exercise personal power.[6] The *paterfamilias,* the head of the household, has the right to exercise his will relative to others in the household. The recurring imagery in this characterization of authority sanctifies the personal power of the person in charge. In religious terms, as Weber and others noted, a person obtains the right to personal power through his singular ability to reach out to touch a higher level of truth, a transcendental level. In Antiquity, the patriarch served as the family priest and the patrimonial ruler as a deity himself (variations that Weber called hierocracy, theocracy, and Caesaropapism) among other deities aiding the empire, all various forms of divine right (Weber, 1978: 1159). This imagery is conveyed clearly in Raphael's painting, shown in Figure 2.

Initially embedded in patriarchal legitimacy, this imagery careens through Western history and has continued potency even today. In a particularly insightful essay, Robert Bellah (1970) compares the father-and-son relationships in Christian and Confucian cultures. He (1970: 82) shows that in Christianity the images of the father–son relationship 'emerge in the first instance from the Christian notion of God, around which the whole symbolic structure hangs.' In this imagery, authority is viewed as originating with God, who is the 'unmoved mover,' the ultimate cause of which everything else is an effect. Biology is detached from this imagery. 'The Christian attitude toward political and familial authority', Bellah (1970: 92) writes, is 'based on the premise of the derivative nature of such authority,' and it is on this basis, and not biology, that 'parents and rulers should be reverenced.'

With this imagery, power is portrayed as a positive force, a force that emanates from the will of a superior person, whose right to exercise his or her will is derived from and justified by a higher source of authority, be that God or natural law or the will of the people. 'In the West,' says Bellah (1970: 92), 'from the time of Mosaic revelation, every particular pattern of social relations was in principle derived of ultimacy... In the West it was God alone who in the last analysis exercised power.' Touched by the ultimate, people, and not positions or roles, served as the focus of Western imagery. Salvation, freedom, reason, contract are all ideas involving people exercising their will, and, like straws in a haystack, each person

---

[6] Weber repeatedly emphasized the personal power inherent in traditional authority. Weber's most analytical statement on this issue come in his discussion of the 'pure type' of traditional authority (1978: 227). This is a particularly important discussion, because it lays out the theoretical foundation of his typology of traditional authority. Herein Weber defined what he called the 'double sphere' of traditional authority, which ties action, on the one hand, to 'specific traditions' and, on the other hand, to the personal prerogatives of the master, who is 'free of specific rules.'

in the same organizational unit can use the same vocabulary of rights and duties to justify their actions.

Cast as the willed acts of the empowered, domination then logically requires jurisdictions within which one's personal power is deemed legitimate, and outside of which it is deemed illegitimate because such power would conflict with the prerogatives of others. In the West, most conflicts over whose authority should prevail are, in fact, jurisdictional conflicts. For example, patriarchalism declined in the West not because the heads of household lost their authority absolutely, but rather because their jurisdictions shrank, and their rights within those jurisdictions reduced, relative to those of other legitimate holders of power. Outside the household, Western rulers claimed jurisdiction over all subjects in the realm, including those within patriarchal households. Within the household, Protestantism allowed children and wives to claim their own right to disobey their earthly patriarch in favor of a father of a higher order. 'Our Father who art in Heaven' gave people access to a stand of principled disobedience, a stand that continually upholds the jurisdictional premises of Western power, even as it challenges the exact boundaries of jurisdictions themselves.

Chinese Authority as Legitimate Roles

In the very same way a line-and-block chart delineates a structure of authority, *patria potestas* signifies the power of persons in positions. By contrast, *xiao* signifies the obedience of persons to the duties embedded in the subordinate roles they occupy. Like the waves (*lun*伦) coming out from the core, *xiao* is a doctrine that defines a series of dyadic relationships and identifies the obligations to fulfill the role of the subordinate in those relationships.[7] The son has the obligation to act as a son in relation to his parents, regardless of his will or of his situation in life or even of whether his parents are alive or not. The obligation to submit to roles continues regardless of circumstances, and no person is exempt from the necessity to fulfill the obligations of their roles, even the Chinese emperor, who is the Son of Heaven and who is, in principle, obligated to fill that role, as well as to be a son to his parents.

The *Xiaojing* (《孝经》), *The Book of Filial Piety*, is the classic text on the meaning of *xiao*.[8] Most likely written in the earliest years of the Han dynasty (200 BC–220AD), the *Xiaojing* is a short book of aphorisms, 18 chapters in all, about two thousand characters in length. The character for *xiao* signifies serving one's parents, but in the *Xiaojing* this concept is elevated to mean obedience to roles in general. Everything and everyone, without exception, has a role to fulfill; otherwise things fall apart. The first chapter states the overarching premise: '*Xiao* is the foundation of virtue and the root of civilization.' Although '*xiao* begins in

---

[7] For the detailed discussion of *xiao*, see Hamilton (1984), but see Holzman's excellent analysis (1998) as well.

[8] For the passages below, I use Mary Lelia Makra's translation of the *Xiaojing* (1970).

the service of parents,' it extends out to encompass everyone. The ruler, the Son of Heaven, has his *xiao* (chapter two), the nobility has its *xiao* (chapter three), the administrators have their *xiao* (chapter four), all the way down to the common people, who have their *xiao* as well (chapter six).

The imagery is unequivocal. All humans have their roles to fulfill, but so does everything else too. The heaven and the earth have respective roles to which they must adhere, and so, too, does mankind (chapter seven). Submission to roles is the order of things, and it is through submission to one's own roles that the world avoids calamities (chapter eleven). Roles are dyadic in nature, and each dyad finds its expression in the duties of the subordinate to the superior. The superior in a dyad governs the subordinate by him- or herself setting an example of being dutiful to his own roles requiring submission. A father owes *xiao* to his own father. The emperor rules the empire through exemplary behavior, being filial to his own parents and being dutiful as the Son of Heaven. Roles are an inherent part of the order of things, in the human, as well as in the non-human world. Embedded in roles are both the normative principles and the prescriptive duties that the subordinate should feel and do. These principles and duties exist regardless of who occupies the role of the superior or what that person does.

The key point here is that *xiao* means obedience to the subordinate's role and not obedience to the superior's commands. The *Xiaojing* makes this point clear in chapter 15:

> The Master's disciple inquires, 'Dare I ask if a son, by obeying all of this father's command, can be called *xiao*.' The Master answered: 'How can you say that? … In the case of contemplated moral wrong, a son must never fail to warn his father against it; nor must a minister fail to perform a like service for his prince. In short, when there is a question of moral wrong, there should be correction. How can you say that *xiao* consists in simply obeying a father?'

Nowhere in the discussion of *xiao,* either in the *Xiaojing* or in any other canonical texts of Chinese civilization, is there a place for the legitimate exercise of personal power. In fact, quite the opposite theme prevails. Humanness is found only in the careful cultivation of roles and of finding the personhood in the roles themselves. This theme is the essence of Confucianism. With *patria potestas* it is the person and not the role that is valorized; with *xiao* it is the person in the role that is praised. With *xiao*, humanness requires the denial of strictly individual desires and unique selves, and, more importantly, *xiao* requires the studied negation of personal magic, the negation of charisma, the very spirit that the West tried to corral through creating jurisdictions.

The core and enduring difference between *xiao* and *patria potestas* is addressed in Bellah's comparison. Although patriarchy and patrilineality look similar in both China and the West until the modern era, Bellah finds the Chinese image of the father–son relationship 'differs radically from that image in Judaism and Christianity.' 'When we look at the Confucian attitude toward political and familial authority, there is no point of leverage in the Confucian symbol system from which disobedience to parents could be justified.' (1970: 84). The Chinese had no 'God the Father, who art in Heaven,' no transcendental level where a greater reality could be found and where earthly power could be justified. Instead, domination was legitimated through an immanent justification.

The Chinese cosmos portrayed the immanent nature of all things. Heaven, earth, and man are distinct parts of the whole, and each has its own nature and its own roles in maintaining the stability of the whole from time immemorial. Joseph Needham (1956: 287) described the Chinese cosmos as a 'an ordered harmony of wills without an ordainer; it was like the spontaneous yet ordered... movement of dancers... none of whom are bound by law to do what they do, nor yet pushed by others coming behind, but cooperate in a voluntary harmony of wills.' Needham (1956: 287) contrasted the Chinese harmony of wills with a depiction of the West as the clashing of wills, like 'the physical clash of innumerable billiard balls in which the motion of the one was the physical cause of the impulsion of the other' with God being the Unmoved Mover.

In the Chinese cosmos, in principle, there are no commands, just obedience. An ancient commentary on the *I Ching* notes: 'We do not see Heaven command the four seasons, and yet they never swerve from their course. So also we do not see the sage ordering the people about, and yet they obey and spontaneously serve him' (Needham 1956: 561–562). By making the performance of duties necessary to the proper functioning of the whole, the powerful grounded their own prerogatives in the duties of their own roles, which allowed them to hold subordinates to the duties of their respective roles. As Bellah concludes, in Confucian imagery 'submission [was] not in the last analysis to a person but to a *pattern* of personal relationships that is held to have ultimate validity' (1970: 84).

Some Empirical Evidence Supporting the Theory

In suggesting that *patria potestas* and *xiao* represent very different principles of legitimate domination, I am making the same point that Fei makes: These are not merely theoretical differences, but also empirical differences. In other words, if the theory is correct and the analogies are useful, then there should be empirical evidence that substantiates the differences. To demonstrate the plausibility of his theory, from chapter five on in *Xiangtu Zhongguo*, Fei showed empirically how the analogies apply to real life. Similarly, in previous writing, I made three sets of empirical comparisons between China and the West (1980, 1990). In each of the tests, I selected an institutionalized sphere of activity associated with Western patriarchalism and patrimonialism and showed that the comparable sphere of activity in China differed from that in the West. Moreover, the Chinese equivalent could be better explained by the relational premises associated with *xiao*. The first test employs the temporal dimension associated with *patria potestas*. According to Weber, and also to others, patriarchalism as a legitimate principle of domination prevailed throughout the Mediterranean basin during Antiquity, but gradually lessened as time passed (1990: 85–88). The empirical point of interest is the right of a patriarch to punish his wife or children, even to death, for cause, a legal principle called *ius vitae necisque*. Even though it is debatable how much this right was actually used, it is clear that *ius vitae necisque* was recognized, in principle, as a legitimate act throughout the Mediterranean region well into the Roman era, when the right was revoked and when the Roman rulers claimed those powers for themselves and denied the right to all others (Thompson 2006). If we use *ius vitae necisque* as a measure of patriarchal power, then we can argue that patriarchy was stronger in ancient times[9] than it was in later periods. Moreover, we can explain the termination of *ius vitae necisque* as the outcome of a jurisdictional conflict with regard to who had authority over the life and death of people within the household. By the late fourth century AD, Roman emperors claimed for themselves the right of life and death over all subjects. After that time, the powers of heads of household became increasingly circumscribed relative to patrimonial powers of rulers and the feudal aristocracy. Once we reach the early modern era, Western patriarchalism has so reduced its jurisdictional sway that it is associated only with the legally specified powers of fathers over wives and children in nuclear families.

In China, fathers also had the right to punish their children to death, but the timeline is reversed. From the earliest times through the Tang (618–906 AD) and Song (960–1279) dynasties, killing one's children or wives, for whatever reason, was strictly forbidden (Qu 1961: 19). But in China's last two dynasties, during the Ming (1368–1644) and the Qing (1644–1911) periods, parents would go unpunished if they killed their son for being unfilial. During these last dynasties, the legal codes increasingly specified the behavior that was unfilial and greatly strengthened the father's authority over his sons and his wives with regard to unfiliality. By Ming times, the increasingly harsh reading of Chinese legal codes, which had been carried forward from the Tang dynasty, allowed parents to prosecute their children in the magistrate's court and even to ask for the child's death. *Qu* notes that 'the government merely acted as agent, framed the regulations and saw to it that they were carried out' (1961: 27).

What explains this increasing ability of fathers and husbands to punish their wives and children for lacking *xiao*? There is no evidence that the rulers during the Ming and Qing periods were weak. Quite the contrary is true (e.g., Spence 1975). But there is every reason to think that, as *xiao* became rationalized during the course of China's long history, the essential roles (the three bonds, *sangang* (三纲), and the five relationships *wulun* (五伦): father/son, husband/wife, ruler/official, older brother/younger brother, and friends) became increasingly typified and more rigorously enforced in the last two dynasties. This rationalization occurred

---

[9] Remember the biblical story of Abraham and Isaac.

in conjunction with the reinterpretation and reinforcement of Confucianism as the official doctrine legitimating the Chinese imperial rule. This movement, known as Neo-Confucianism, started in the Song Dynasty, with variations continuing to the end of the Qing period. With Neo-Confucianism came a new emphasis on the *sangang* and *wulun*, and a new sense of *xiao* as a virtue that stabilized the empire. This explanation gains substance with the next two sets of comparisons.

The second test looks at the configuration of the household (1990: 88–92). *Patria potestas* refers to the authority of the head of household over all aspects of the household, including slaves. Owning slaves, and counting them as property of the household, was commonplace throughout the Mediterranean region. As Weber noted, the household in Antiquity was the *oikos*, an extended patrilineal territory that was at once the basic economic and political unit of the region. As described by Aristotle in *Politics*, and as Weber (1976) carefully compared throughout the Mediterranean, the *oikos* was a 'strongly tradition-bound structure of domination… the manor (*seigneurie*), joining lord and manorial dependent with ties that cannot be dissolved unilaterally' (Weber 1978: 1012). The *oikos* estates centered on the power of the head of household to control both his property and his dependants. In Roman law, the essence of *patria potestas* was the *paterfamilias'* ability to control and to perpetuate this extended household. Despite some attenuation, this power continued in the West through the early modern period, ending only with the development of capitalism in modern times.

In China, however, *oikos*-like estates, including slavery and peasants bound to the soil, occurred in the earlier dynasties, but were not widely present in the Ming or Qing periods. Even though the authority of the father relative to his wives and children increased in late imperial China, that authority did not extend beyond close family members. Slavery was widespread in China from ancient times to the Tang dynasty; large manors, with peasants bound to the soil were commonplace in the Song period; but in the Ming dynasty, as the parent/child relationship became more rigidly defined, heads of household lost the ability to extend that power beyond the immediate kinship group. Moreover, peasants increasingly became free peasants who paid rent, who claimed the rights to the topsoil, and who engaged in market transactions independent of their landlords (Rowe 1985; Eastman 1988).

Clearly, the *oikos* configuration in China does not line up with the father's ability to punish his children, as it does in the West. Predictions based on the developmental trends occurring in Western Europe simply do not hold up for China. This misalignment suggests that the nature of domination in China became increasingly less personal, less arbitrary, and more fixed on rationalizing behavior in roles.[10]

---

[10] Paradoxically, the developmental trends in the West also became increasingly less personal, less arbitrary, and more fixed on rationalizing individual behavior; only in the West, legitimacy rationalized around laws rather than roles.

The third test is perhaps the most decisive (1989). If the legitimating principle of domination in China is not based on the ability to exercise personal power within a jurisdiction, then the organization of patrimonial rule in the West and China should differ. Patrimonial rule in China should rest on the principle of *xiao*, on obedience to roles. To simplify matters greatly, we can characterize the organization of Western states, including patrimonial states, as consisting of three features: first, a centrist conception of legitimate power, which is focused on the person who has the right to issue commands; second, a 'top–down' administrative organization, consisting of a chain of command through which a staff carries out the lawful commands of the power holder; and, third, a legitimate jurisdiction within which the leader's commands are valid and outside of which they are invalid. This characterization is very much in line with Weber's conception of an organized system of domination, as he stated explicitly in his essay 'Politics as a Vocation' (1946), and as he developed extensively through his writings. Moreover, this is *tuantigeju*, writ large, applied to China.

I have argued that the organization of the Chinese state during the late imperial period differs substantially from these three features of Western states (1989, 1990). First, political organization in China was not organized as an administrative structure. Instead, the Chinese state is organized as a status hierarchy. By status hierarchy, I mean an organization consisting of hierarchically arranged sets of roles that are largely self-contained and which are not linked by an explicit command structure.[11] We can think of this organization as being symbolized by the intricately carved set of Chinese ivory balls, which has one free-floating ball inside another inside another, or the Chinese nesting boxes, which are a box within a box within a box, as a circle within a circle within a circle. The Chinese status order consists of a core status group, surrounded by another status group, surrounded by yet another group. The commoners form the symbolic center, the officials and other administrators are in the middle, and the emperor and the imperial household, the outermost status group, surround China. As a familiar Chinese saying notes ('Heaven is high and the emperor is far away'), the imperial realm is conceptualized as being far removed from the commoners and located next to heaven, which is a fitting location for the Son of Heaven, who has the 'mandate of heaven.'

Each status group consisted of people who had roles requiring obligation: commoners needed to serve their parents, officials needed to serve the emperor and his household, and the emperor and his household needed to serve heaven.

---

[11] An example of a similarly organized order in the West are universities. Students, faculty, and administrators form distinct categories of individuals; different rules and regulations apply to each category, along with a different sort of social honor. Within universities there is, in theory, no unity of command, no sense that the person in charge of the university has the right to issue direct commands to individuals in the other groups. Instead, as a system of control, the university enforces a different set of rules for each group, and in principle each group is self-governing through a regulatory body appropriate for the group.

Each status group maintained a substantial gap separating members of the superior group from members of the subordinate groups, so much so that, as time went on, there was very little formal contact between groups. Most contacts between groups were handled by intermediaries classified as outsiders (*wairen* 外人), mean people (*jianmin* 贱民) who did not fit within the status system: eunuchs, *yamen* runners, bondservants, household slaves (Hamilton 1989).

In Western political organization, individuals in positions of power have the right, even the obligation, to transmit their will to others within their jurisdiction. Leaders have to lead. But in Chinese political organization, the primary mode of maintaining hierarchy is not through command, but through self-cultivation (being aware of appropriate behavior for yourself) and correction (holding others to their correct roles). This idea is conveyed in the very word for government itself, a combination of two characters, *zhengzhi* (政治). *Zheng* (政) consists of two parts: the root component means correct or appropriate behavior, to be true to form; and the second component of the character means to follow. *Zhi* (治), the second character in the combination, means to heal or to cure. *Zhengzhi* provides the image of domination in China: The powers that be are to follow correct behavior themselves and to set right that which is incorrect among subordinates.

This image of correct rule permeated the daily practices of China's imperial rulers. For instance, Chinese emperors did not issue commands as such, but rather imperial edicts. In classifying these edicts, Leon Vandermeersch noted that, in China, these categories of sovereign decisions 'in no way denote[s] positive laws; [they] refer to the fundamental laws of nature insofar as these are models for the right conduct of government' (1985: 13). He contrasts the Western notion of law with the Chinese notion of ritual order:

> The principle of ritual order is... modeled upon forms – rites – which are the reasons (*li* 理, principles) of things. Only in conformity with those reasons can the world function harmoniously. Once the rites have been respected, and harmony has thereby been introduced into society, each individual spontaneously behaves as is most fitting for all and for himself.... People are persuaded to subject themselves to the rites by the prestige and the imposing forms of the greatest ceremonies, and by the ascendancy, and the example, of the highest personages of the social hierarchy. This is why the most important edicts are those which concern great liturgical celebrations and those which involve great dignitaries.... The Chinese, after all, have always upheld as their model the administrator who never intervenes in the affairs of those whom he administers, the latter acting under the influence of his virtue, in spontaneous conformity with the norms of the social order.

These three 'tests' of the difference between the premises of legitimacy in the West and China are merely suggestive. Fei's empirical comparisons between Western and Chinese societies are also suggestive. However, what both sets of comparisons suggest is that, despite difficulties in making cross-civilizational comparisons, there are genuine differences in the principles of legitimate domination between China and the West. Moreover, these differences point to the fact the distinctive legitimate principle of domination in each society directly shapes how institutionalized spheres of activity came to be organized.

Conclusion

Although greatly abbreviated here, the empirical evidence suggests that Western and Chinese principles of legitimate domination are different and embody different empirical configurations. To the extent that this paper is correct and that these differences can be empirically substantiated, then we should not equate Chinese and Western political and social institutions, as social scientists often do. We should recognize the brilliance of Fei's initial insights and see them as civilizational images of legitimate authority, images that have had direct and persistent effects on how social activity has been routinely organized. Fei's insights need to be refined and tested far beyond what analysts have done to date. Only then can we ask the question that needs to be answered: To what extent has *chaxugeju* persisted today after the great changes that China has gone through in the most recent century? Equally we can ask the same question of the West. Have the images embedded in the Western patriarchalism of old survived the transformative changes the West has gone through, and, if so, in what form? Is it a reasonable hypothesis to suggest that Weber's analysis of the West and Fei's analysis of Chinese society are both persistent forms of social organization and continue on into our own time? Can we hypothesize that legal rational domination, as described by Weber, represents a radical transformation of Western patriarchy, a transformation that has allowed all people equal access to law and to God? Can we not also hypothesize that *xiao*, likewise, has modern manifestations that have survived the onslaught of modernization? These are important questions to study because the answers show the way to a deeper understanding of our times.

Fei's analysis also suggests that social scientists around the world blithely use an array of concepts that have civilizational meanings without the least awareness that these concepts contain, typically, a Eurocentric bias. Unlike in mathematics, parsimony in social science leads to mistakes. All similarly located institutions may not be equivalent, even within the same civilizational areas. To use concepts carelessly is to distort the subject matter of the very world of activity that we want to study. To further obscure these concepts in the pseudo-scientific whirl of methodological exactitude is to lead social scientists away from a rigorous understanding of their own society. In *Xiangtu Zhongguo*, Fei is calling for concepts that are methodologically adequate for the study of China, and warns in *Xiangtu Chongjian* that the use of Western concepts to analyze Chinese society may have pernicious results. This is a warning that we still need to hear and to heed.

References

Bellah, Robert. 1970. *Beyond Belief.* New York: Harper and Row.

Chan, Alan K.L. and Tan, Sor-Hoon Eds. 2004. *Filial Piety in Chinese Thought and History.* Singapore: Routledge, Curzon.

Eastman, Lloyd E. 1988. *Family, Field, and Ancestors: Constancy and Change in China's Social and Economic History, 1550-1949.* Oxford: Oxford University Press.

费孝通:《乡土中国》, 北京: 三联书店, 1985年重印 [(Fei, Xiaotong. 1985[1947]. *Xiangtu Zhongguo* (in Chinese), Beijing: SDX Joint Publishing Company)].

— 1992. *From the Soil: The Foundations of Chinese Society.* Translation of Fei Xiaotong's *Xiangtu Zhongguo* with an introduction and epilogue by Gary Hamilton and Wang Zheng, Berkeley: University of California Press.

Hamilton, Gary. 1984. 'Patriarchalism in Imperial China and Western Europe: A Revision of Weber's Sociology of Domination', *Theory and Society* 13 (May): 393-426.

— 1989. 'Heaven is High and the Emperor is Far Away', *Revue europeenne des sciences sociales* 27: 141-167.

— 1990. 'Patriarchy, Patrimonialism and Filial Piety: A Comparison of China and Western Europe', *British Journal of Sociology* 41 (March): 77-104.

— 2006. *Commerce and Capitalism in Chinese Societies.* London: Routledge.

Hamilton, Gary and Kao Cheng-shu. 2009. 'The Round Table: A Reconsideration of Chinese Business Networks.' In E. Sinn, Wong Siu-lun, Chan Wing-hoi. Eds. *Rethinking Hong Kong; New Paradigms, New Perspectives.* Hong Kong: Centre of Asian Studies, The University of Hong Kong.

Holzman, Donald. 1998. 'The Place of Filial Piety in Ancient China', *Journal of the American Oriental Society* 118, 2 (April-June): 185-199.

Ikels, Charlotte. Ed. 2004. *Filial Piety: Practice and Discourse in Contemporary East Asia.* Stanford: Stanford University Press.

Makra, Mary L. (Trans.). 1970. *Xiaojing.* New York: St. John's University Press.

Needham, Joseph. 1956. *Science and Civilization in China.* Vol. 2. Cambridge: Cambridge University Press.

Qu Tongzu (Ch'u T'ung-tsu). 1961. *Law and Society in Traditional China.* Paris: Monton.

Rowe, William T. 1985. 'Approaches to Modern Chinese Social History', in Olivier Zunz. Ed. *Reliving the Past: The Worlds of Social History,* pp. 236-296. Chapel Hill: University of North Carolina Press.

Schluchter, Wolfgang. 1989. *Rationalism, Religion and Domination. A Weberian Perspective.* Berkeley: University of California Press.

Spence, Jonathan D. 1975. *Emperor of China: Self Portrait of K'ang-Hsi.* New York: Vintage Books.

Swidler, Ann. 1986. 'Culture in Action: Symbols and Strategies', *American Sociological Review* 51 (April):273-286.

Thompson, Steven. 2006. 'Was Ancient Rome a Dead Wives Society? What Did the Roman Paterfamilias Get Away With?' *Journal of Family History* 31, 3 (January):3-27.

Turner, Karen. 1993. 'War, Punishment, and the Law of Nature in Early Chinese Concepts of the State'. *Harvard Journal of Asiatic Studies* 53, 2 (December), 284-324.

Turner, Karen, Feinerman, James V., Guy, R. Kent. 2000. *The Limits of the Rule of Law in China.* Seattle: University of Washington Press.

Vandermeersch, Léon. 1985. 'An Enquiry into the Chinese Conception of the Law', in Stuart R. Schram. Ed. *The Scope of State Power in China.* Hong Kong: The Chinese University of Hong Kong Press.

Weber, Max. 1976[1909]. *The Agrarian Sociology of Ancient Civilizations.* Trans. R.I. Frank. London: Verso.

— 1951[1920]. *The Religion of China.* Trans. and ed. H. Gerth. Glencoe, Ill.: Free Press.

— 1978[1921-22]. *Economy and Society.* Trans. and ed. G. Roth and C. Wittich. 3 vols. Berkeley: University of California Press.

— 1946. *From Max Weber: Essays in Sociology.* Trans, ed., and with an introduction by H.H. Gerth and C. Wright Mills. New York: Oxford University Press.

— 1958[1904-5]. *The Protestant Ethic and the Spirit of Capitalism.* Trans. T. Parsons. New York: Charles Scribner's Sons.

阎云翔：《网络社会的道德等级和社会利己主义：重读费孝通〈差序格局〉一文》，见王斯福、常向群和周大鸣主编《中国社会科学全球化—费孝通诞辰一百零五周年纪念文集》，新世界出版社和全球中国出版社,2015年版

Yan, Yunxiang. 'Moral Hierarchy and Social Egoism in a Networked Society: The Chaxugeju Thesis Revisited', in Feuchtwang, S; Chang, X. and Zhou, D. Eds. *Globalization of Chinese Social Science – Commemorate the 100th Anniversary of Professor Fei Xiaotong's Birth*, published jointly published by Global China Press and New World Press, 2015.

DOI https://doi.org/10.24103/GCSS1.en.2015.6

Social Egoism and Individualism: Surprises and Questions for a Western Anthropologist of China Reading Professor Fei Xiaotong's Contrast Between China and the West[1]

Stephan Feuchtwang

Abstract: This paper comments on the cultural comparisons between China and the West made in Fei Xiaotong's book, *From the Soil: The Foundations of Chinese Society*, and asserts the important significance of Fei's concept of "differential mode of association" in Chinese sociological and anthropological studies as well as in any attempt at China–West cultural comparisons. On the basis of that, the author revises the contrast between egoism and individualism by pointing out that, as the importance of economic relations is growing rapidly and extensively, a new differential mode of association is evolving to include trust between neighbours, friends and families, and the pursuit of common interests. It is also broadening into a way of conducting business transactions and political coalitions. The author then goes on to raise the question of how rural China, with social egoism as its defining character, should build up the idea of equal rights and individualism as required by the market economy in its transformational period.

Keywords: social egoism, individualism, *chaxugeju, tuantigeju*, anthropology of China, emotional family in China

My principal subject is the book *Xiangtu Zhongguo*, which Professor Fei wrote in the 1940s, when China was changing very dramatically and amidst great violence. China has changed a lot more since then and so have social anthropology and sociology. I shall offer some observations on these changes. But first I want to

---

[1] This article was originally written for a conference celebrating Fei Xiaotong's 70th anniversary of his academic career and the establishment of the 20th anniversary of the Institute of Sociology and Anthropology at Peking University in 2005. It was then delivered at Department of Sociology, China Agricultural University on the 31st Oct. 2005, and was translated into Chinese by Gong Haoqun and Yang Qingqing, proofread by Zhao Xudong, and published in *Open Times* (Kaifang Shidai), 2009(03): 67–82. The English version was published in Ma Gong, Liu Shiding, Qu Dongqi, and Pan Naigu, eds. *Fei Xiaotong yu Zhongguo Shehuixui Renleixue* (Fei Xiaotong and Chinese Sociology and Anthropology, Social Science Academic Press, 2009:18-32). The author made minor corrections before the English version was published at JCCP, whereas the Chinese version has been updated thoroughly including additional translations based on both the latest English version and the published Chinese version by Julia Yu Du.

pay my respects to this work, which I read in its English translation with pleasant surprise and admiration.

The first and only English translation of *Xiangtu Zhongguo* was published in 1992 under the title '*From the soil: The Foundations of Chinese Society*' (translation, introduction and epilogue by Gary G. Hamilton and Wang Zheng 1992, University of California Press). As the translators point out, Professor Fei was writing about rural China but treating it as the way Chinese society as a whole works. They stress that Fei wrote for an urban readership that was in the midst of change and was looking to the West and to the Soviet Union to find solutions to China's many problems, including recovery from Japanese invasion and civil war. Fei wrote *Xiangtu Chongjian* (*Reconstructing Rural China*) at the same time. Putting them together shows that he wanted any rebuilding of China to be based on what it already was, rather than to recommend a complete transformation based on urban China and using imported ideas, which would inevitably do further violence and would fail. So he wrote *Xiangtu Zhongguo* to establish what China already was. What China was and remained at that time was agrarian and rural.

Addressing his urban readership, Fei took on the task of showing that ideas imported from the West were inappropriate, because they came from and were appropriate to a completely different kind of society and its culture. He was then able, in *Xiangtu Chongjian*, to say how China could industrialize and build a modern state and society on a completely different basis from that of the pre-industrial West, because he had in fact made two comparisons, between agrarian and industrial society in general, and between Western and Chinese cultures in particular.

Xiangtu Zhongguo is a sustained comparison of two very different societies, one of which is his own. Fei's comparison is based on personal experience and research. He had lived for about two years in the UK and about a year in the USA and had read books of sociological research on US society by US sociologists. Indeed he published a third book on *The American Character* (*Meiguoren de Xingge*, Shanghai: Shenghuo) in 1947. So both sides of the comparison were empirically well informed. This was and still is unusual. But even less usual is the fact that it is a view of Western society by an outsider, whereas the usual comparison is by Western social scientists of their own society with the non-Western societies that they have studied.

I am a Western anthropologist and sociologist who studies Chinese society, so I am coming to Professor Fei's work from the opposite direction. I study China as an outsider and bring to the comparison with the West my own reading of sociological and anthropological studies of the UK and the USA. Of course I am also bringing to the comparison my reading of studies of both China and the West (UK and USA) that Fei could not have read in the 1940s. They indicate many social changes since then on both sides of the comparison. I will have some remarks to offer on the changes that have occurred in both our societies since *Xiangtu Zhongguo*, and on changes that have occurred in the anthropology of some of the topics that are of central importance for Fei. But first I want to comment on how I came to know about *Xiangtu Zhongguo*.

On the anthropology of China in the UK in the 1960s

When I was being introduced to the anthropology of China, I read Fei's village study, *Peasant Life in China* (1939), his studies with Zhang Zhiyi whose English title is *Earthbound China* (1949), and his book on *China's Gentry* (1953). I did not realize then that the book on *China's Gentry* was made out of some chapters from *Xiangtu Chongjian*. This was because I read what had been translated into English in the 1960s. Now, when I teach the anthropology of China, at the London School of Economics (LSE), I ask students to read *Xiangtu Zhongguo* in translation. This is because I think serious comparative work is very important, whereas when I was learning to be an anthropologist in the sixties, what my teachers and I thought was most important was learning about other people, and comparing them, but leaving the comparison with our own societies as an implicit by-product of writing in English.

There was something else involved too. We read a number of studies by Chinese sociologists and anthropologists, but we read them for the information they provided about Chinese culture and society, including Chinese ideas about how to conduct themselves and about the world from their point of view. We did not read them as the products of a Chinese social science, by fellow theorists.

This is odd, because my teacher, Maurice Freedman, had rightly written in 1961 that 'outside North America and Western Europe, China was the seat of the most flourishing sociology' (1979: 379). He did not have available to him in translation the more general, theorizing books by the social scientists he so admired, including Professor Fei. Maurice Freedman did not read Chinese well enough; he could only speak Hokkien. I could read Chinese, but neither of us knew about *Xiangtu Zhongguo*: the result was ignorance about Chinese social scientists' theories on Chinese society. The translation of *Xiangtu Zhongguo* in 1992 by Gary Hamilton and Wang Zheng is the result of a new time of mutual respect and co-operation between Western and Chinese social scientists, although it is still rather one-sided because the Chinese anthropologists and sociologists with whom we Westerners work most closely have spent years in Western universities. It is still very rare for a Western sociologist or anthropologist to study social sciences in China. But it is beginning to happen. At the same time, I am very aware that there is a continuing imbalance of resources and concentration of research and comparison, such that even now English is the main language of publication in international sociology and anthropology, and I am lecturing in English even though I am here, in China. Coming from the LSE, one of Fei's mother universities (alma mater, *muxiao*), which advertises itself as a world centre and a unique concentration of social scientific research and teaching, I am conscious of being in a privileged position. Even so, I think this *is* a time for greater mutual respect and self-questioning among colleagues, wherever they are centred, retaining what my friend and colleague Wang Mingming has called 'the third eye' of anthropology (2002).

In any case, at the level of concept if not general theory in social science, the type of sociality binding Chinese rural society in Fei's conception is *chaxugeju* ('differential mode of association' in Hamilton and Wang's translation). I am translating it as 'social egoism' to capture his point that each ring of association differs according to the position of the person who makes those rings. Reading about this concept came to me as a great surprise, because of my education under Maurice Freedman.

Corporate group versus small lineage

In British anthropology at the time when I studied with Freedman, the idea of social structure was an abstraction from what could be observed. The abstraction was a model of what might be the rules and principles of social organization and individual conduct, to be tested by further observation. British anthropologists like Freedman likened the rules and principles to laws. These were not physical laws; they were social laws, which he called 'jural' (Freedman 1970: 373–379). But they were not identified with written or stated laws. When as in China there were sets of written laws or codes, they were treated as indications of underlying and more general principles and rules of organization and conduct.

Fei's *chaxugeju* was also an abstraction and a model of observable and historically described Chinese society. He freely used his personal observations on one hand and quotations from Confucian classics on the other hand, to model a structure of Chinese society that had not itself changed in two thousand years, despite the changes he saw going on around him and which he knew had occurred in a longer historical time frame.

Both Freedman and Fei modelled what they proposed to be a basic structure that needed to be understood first, before they could write about social change.

I did the same later when I wrote *The Imperial Metaphor* (1992), but it was not about Chinese society as a whole. It was a conception of what I took to be a basic institution of Chinese social life, the institution of territorial protector cults and their festivals, even though I knew I was observing them under a process of profound change. An institution sometimes means an organization, but not here. I was following another British anthropologist of Maurice Freedman's generation, S.F. Nadel (1951: ch. 6). For Nadel, a social institution is not a group or an organization, with a membership, rules of recruitment, and a boundary. It is a series of actions, patterned and with linked aims, performed regularly, such as the institution of marriage, or the institution of rites of passage, or the institution of the law, or of monarchy, or of kinship.

The distinction between institution and organization is interesting, but there is a more fascinating difference between Fei's and Freedman's models.

Freedman produced a model of Chinese kinship both as institution and as organization of groups, lineages and families, stressing rules of membership and recruitment. In my attempt to establish the universality in China of the institution of territorial cults, I did not stress membership and recruitment. Instead, I emphasized territorial boundaries and the distinction between inside and outside.

Freedman's was a model of corporate groups, lineages, which segment and grow in power according to their relations with the state and their different property holdings. He made a sharp distinction between family and lineage. Family is a more transient group, whereas a lineage is in principle permanent because it is defined as descent from a known ancestor. Fei's model, by contrast, was of the circles of social relatedness spreading out from each social person, so that he calls a family a small lineage. It is an efficient, flexible and expandable, multi-functional organization. For both Freedman and Fei, the household is a transient organization, but Fei pointed out that a family household was already a unit of lineal descent, presenting an organizational form that varied according to different purposes or functions. For Fei it was vital to conceive of sociality, starting from the family, as ego-centred, whereas for Freedman and in the studies of kinship in English anthropology in Freedman's time, ego-centred kinship was known as 'kindred' and was distinguished from a permanent structure. Kindred in contrast to lineage, is transient precisely because it is ego-centred. For Fei, ego-centred kinship is both transient and permanent. Freedman's lasting organization is conceived of as a group, whereas Fei's lasting organization has no fixed boundaries. It certainly has rules, lawlike customary rules, but it precedes either organization or institution as a primary conception of sociality. For Fei, 'structure' in the English anthropological sense of something permanent and fixed, would be too abstract.

Similarly to this stress on permanent and fixed organization, in European languages 'society' is usually understood as a large group, or a group of groups. There is also the adjective 'social', which can be turned into a noun 'the social', which is understood to be social relations in general and the obligations that bind it. But in the tradition of Durkheim, and therefore of British anthropology, what binds people to each other is also what binds them into a single society.

The difference between the rural sociology or anthropology that Fei founded in China and the anthropology and sociology that he and Freedman had learned in London and its equivalent in Chicago in the 1930s and 1940s, and which I learned in the 1960s, seems to confirm the contrast Fei made in his sustained comparison. In *Xiangtu Zhongguo*, he says Western society is dominated by a conception of groups and of the individual as a member of a group being like a straw in a haystack, although of course the same straw can be a member of several stacks.

I shall return to the study of kinship and how Fei's concept of Chinese kinship surprised me. But first I want to mention two other surprises that came out of his sustained comparison between the West and China. His comparison is about politics, and first of all about ideals and ideology that are in origin religious. This was a big and instructive surprise for me, because I have spent most of my life studying Chinese religion and politics.

Sage versus God

Fei contrasted a society in which a single universal God represents the universality of public organizations and the principle of law and of love from outside before which everyone is equal, with a society based on sages and ritual or rules of conduct that differentiate. I have to comment that he is making an historical comparison, contrasting Christian society after the Protestant Reformation with Chinese imperial society before the Republic. If he had compared medieval Europe with imperial China he would have had to compare two agrarian and hierarchical societies. But he could have said that European feudal hierarchy was a hierarchy of estates, which are fixed statuses out of which it was not possible to move. They were human collectivities, if not socially organized groups. Differences between people were basic, according to the family into which they were born and the status to which that family belonged. It remains true that this European hierarchy is not the same as *chaxugeju*, which is differentiation not of estates, which are categories of membership, but of persons according to age, generation, sex, loyalty to friends, and subjection to masters and rulers, and the expectation of respect for each other's position in a hierarchy of leadership. Except for the permanent inferiority of women to men and of slaves or outcasts to free men, statuses in agrarian China are positions through which an individual can move. They are not populations in fixed categories.

Fei's social egoism and differentiation, *chaxugeju*, is a hierarchy based on ranked and differentiated social persons, not ranked and differentiated social groups, and he makes this perfectly clear. A person in the course of their lifetime moves from being a child owing obedience to parents, to being a parent expecting obedience, and so on. A person owing loyalty to a leader can eventually become a leader, although most did and do not. In this hierarchy, social statuses are not groups, but of course they do mark themselves off with literacy, long fingernails and other marks of distinction. To make yet another contrast, in the Indian caste hierarchy, social mobility occurs by a process of caste mobility, called Sanskritization, in which a sub-caste or caste moves up as a whole. And medieval European estates of nobles, freemen and serfs were permanently fixed.

Respect for sages of a classical past, for ancestors, and for present elders is, as Fei rightly says, a proposition completely different from a predestination (Protestant) or a fate (Catholic) already decided by a Creator God. A sage whose first priority is filial duty to his father is quite different from a God who is Father to his one Son, born to a virgin human and repudiating his human father so that he can transmit and make flesh God's fatherly love for everyone. A society based on divine law and later on the secular sovereignty of law is quite a contrast to a society based on rules of proper conduct in differentiated roles.

The God of love and justice that induces the ideal of an individual equal to all others before that love and justice, and capable of unmediated communion with God, became the ideal of the various Protestant sects and the root of their rebellions and wars against Catholics in Europe. It was the ideal of the English republican revolution, of the foundation of the first American colonies by northern Europeans, and then, in the politics and the intellectual Enlightenment of Europe that rejected a need for God, it was the ideal of the republican revolutions of France and other countries of continental Europe. The founders of the United States of America were both Enlightened and Protestant. Like most European countries they referred to their God as an authority, yet founded a state that was its own authority and was legitimated by the secular ideals of democracy. Fei's characterization of Western society refers to these, modern Western societies.

His comparison leaves us with two big questions: if the Western countries moved from hierarchies of estates to individualist democracies under the same God, through republican revolutions, what happened to the status differentiation hierarchy of social persons after the republican revolutions in China? How was the social person the basis of a transformed Chinese politics and society? And: What was the effect in China of importing some of the ideals and politics of Western democracy and individualism?

These questions cannot be answered in a short piece. But I will try to indicate directions that their answers could take.

Consensual power and what follows

In *Xiangtu Zhongguo*, Fei argues that in China, as in all settled agrarian societies, the power of the state is dictatorial but limited and that the main form of power is what he calls consensual. Consensual power is the power of association and reputation that can sanction mutual agreement within hierarchical differentiation. Building on his basic model of *chaxugeju*, which is a model of rings of association based on the hierarchical differentiation of consanguinity, this consensual power starts from a strong sense of belonging to where a person is born and will be buried.

For Fei, the sense of belonging to a place is based entirely on consanguinity. I think his emphasis on kinship underestimates the effect of simple territorial neighbourhood, which existed in cities as well as in villages, in China as well as in other agrarian societies. He also underestimates, in my view, the history of lineages displacing previous lineages and of how a sense of not originating form a place is combined with belonging to that place (Zhao 2004). But, bearing in mind these reservations, let me move on to what Fei wrote in the 1940s on consanguinity, local belonging and regionalism, by which he meant association of migrants coming from the same place.

He observed how these relations had been affected by the increasing commercialization of economic relations. He wrote that with increasing monetary transactions, reciprocal (*renqing*) relations would be dominated by the economics of transactions without human sentiments (*wuqing*) and by contractual relationships. But this would not develop naturally into a state of sovereign law creating the space for peaceful transactions and individual rights, as it seemed to him to have done according to the political economy of Adam Smith in Great Britain, through a process of gradual reform. He omits any reference to the violence of the republican civil war in England led by Oliver Cromwell, the terrible vengeance against its leaders by the monarchy that followed the brief English Republic of 1649–1660, and the eventual compromise in the form of the constitutional monarchy established in 1689. I think he is idealizing gradual reform as an aim, by his references to Great Britain. But the idea of gradual reform is an important ideal. Let us see what the alternatives are according to Fei.

The problem for this gradual reform is how a state develops along with the increasing strength of transactions without human sentiments. Fei began reflecting on this problem by referring to modern versions of what he considered to be a primitive form of power, which he called 'temporal power'. Hamilton and Wang comment in a footnote that this is close to or even identical with what Max Weber called 'charismatic authority' (p. 130, fn. 1). Interestingly, Fei's example of a modern form of temporal power, or charismatic authority, was the Soviet Union of his time. He observed that it was prone to disagreements that were not settled by argument and democratic procedures. They were on the one hand suppressed if charismatic power became dictatorial. On the other hand they could turn into disputes between leaders offering different solutions to common problems, which then became power struggles each vying for total ideological control (pp. 131–132). In *Xiangtu Chongjian* he called such power struggles 'factional politics' (quote on p. 145 of Hamilton and Wang). As Hamilton and Wang comment in the chapter they add to their translation of *Xiangtu Zhongguo*, Fei in *Xiangtu Chongjian* (Reconstructing Rural China) hoped for an altogether different result in China. He hoped that the local self-regulation of agrarian China, which was the politics of rule by elders and local gentry, and which was indispensable to the central rule of official bureaucracy from the emperor downwards, could become a new kind of local autonomy based on rural industry. Assemblies of elected representatives would replace local gentry. National government would then have to be a responsive public administration of the central state (pp. 144–145). But of course either path was possible, centralized dictatorial and factional politics, or the politics of central administration checked by local autonomy.

The great difficulty he foresaw would be to create in China a sense of universal public good, and personal responsibility for it. What Hamilton and Wang translate as selfishness, which I am calling social egoism with reference to Fei's typification of Chinese society as *chaxugeju*, is not public social consciousness (p.61). In discussing the concept of generalized humanity and beneficence, *ren*, Fei observes how it was impossible for Confucius to define it. He contrasts it with the Christian idea of love (p. 68), which is also known in English as 'charity', the love of others that induces acts of public individual responsibility and public welfare. More importantly, he contrasts the sharp distinction between the private and the public in Western concepts of civil society with the fluid and indeterminate circles of association starting out from a small lineage. Finally, he contrasts this starting point, which is the first claim on loyalty and the last to be sacrificed, with the demand in the West, often realized, to sacrifice everything for the sake of the state. He must in my opinion have been referring to the national state, not to the agrarian or mercantile empires or even the absolute monarchies of medieval Europe.

The idea of patriotic self-sacrifice and patriotic public good as the supreme social identification, despite different interpretations of what it means, is the hallmark of nationalism. The problem with this ideal is that it becomes a demand that turns into the command of an overbearing state. So the big question that Fei was asking in the 1940s was how could the local autonomy of an agrarian state become an accountable and responsible local leadership within a modern state and grow strong enough to stop the modern, nationalist state of China from being an overbearing top–down power. And the small, but equally important political question he asked was how could primary loyalty to family be developed into a simultaneous social consciousness and responsibility for the public good. It seems to me that these remain very good and important questions to ask. They are basic questions about what Chinese forms of democracy will be.

By the 1940s, the Western ideas of individual rights, the Christian idea of personal conscience, and various models of democratic republican government had already been translated into Chinese writing and put into practice in some institutions, such as provincial assemblies, for half a century (Fincher 1981: ch. 5 and pp. 227–240). But there was still a big question of how they could be made Chinese, which is to say how they could come into a close relationship with rural principles of association and, I would add, rural ideas of territoriality and of responsive and accountable leadership. As I have already pointed out, in my opinion Fei omitted rural ideas of territorial leadership in his stress on consanguinity. There is nothing in *Xiangtu Zhongguo* on territorial cults and the ideas of leadership, public good and social justice that they embody. But within his stress on consanguinity we can certainly find ways of asking more questions about the appropriateness of individualism (*gerenzhuyi*) to Chinese forms of association and family life. In order to do this, I will need to say something about the changes in the study of kinship since the 1940s, and then about changes in Chinese rural society since Fei wrote *Xiangtu Zhongguo*.

Changes in the study of kinship since Professors Fei and Freedman

In the sixties and seventies, the centrality of kinship studies to anthropology in the UK, the USA and France – each with quite different emphases – was challenged so severely that for a time after that the study of kinship seemed to have been abandoned. Kinship had been stressed as the basic structure of the rights and obligations governing the social life of the small states and stateless societies that anthropologists had habitually studied. Freedman had expanded the scope of kinship studies by showing how in the two south-eastern provinces of China, Guangdong and Fujian, asymmetrical segmentation of lineages organized local social life and politics in a large state that was also divided by class (Freedman 1979 [1974]). For him, lineage structure was the context for the social kinship that also organized the relations and the domesticity of family and the alliances between families in marriage. But he made a sharp distinction, as I have already pointed out, between lineage and family, similar to the distinction between jural kinship and biological kinship that his Africanist colleague Meyer Fortes had made.

In 1968, the US anthropologist David Schneider demonstrated the ethnocentricity of the contrast between relations of substance, which is of blood and biology, and coded relations of kinship in law and norms of conduct. He showed that this contrast was characteristic of North American kinship, in which family life is a combination of substance and code, depending on a logically primary distinction between the two. He cast doubt on the universality of this distinction, as it had been assumed until this time in the anthropology of kinship.

As Janet Carsten (2005: 18) comments in her book significantly titled *After Kinship*, Schneider's criticism coincided with a shift away from studies of social structure to studies of cultural meaning, not just in the USA but also in the UK. In the UK this shift made the concept of the person a major focus. And this in turn questioned the assumption, born in Protestant Christianity and reconceived in the European Enlightenment, of the universality of the individual member of organizations, groups and states that Fei had identified as being at the centre of the type of society that he specified as Western: a social system he named *tuantigeju*, which Hamilton and Wang translate as 'the organisational mode of association'.

The most influential studies of the person in the UK from the seventies onwards concentrated not only on meaning but also on the substances of the body, of flows out of, into and between bodies, of gifts and of meals, and of sexual and gender differences. Mary Douglas (*Natural Symbols*, 1970) constructed a typology of all social structures out of the metaphoric use of these substances and flows of the human body. But hers was not a study of the social person in any particular society. Probably the most influential such study in the UK was written by Marilyn Strathern and published in 1988. She contrasted the Melanesian person with Western individualism, just as Fei had contrasted Chinese social egoism with Western individualism, though she knew nothing about Fei's contrast.

The difference between Strathern's and Fei's contrasts is that according to Strathern the Melanesian person is plural and partible. A Melanesian person is a body consubstantial with many others, so that, according to Strathern, it can be conceived of as a social microcosm. Fei does not focus on the body, nor does he deny that the body is individual. Instead he says that a Chinese social person is an individual who is from the start part of a social microcosm, the hierarchically differentiated family, which is a small lineage. For Strathern the Melanesian social person is a result of substantial exchanges, of gifts and meals in rituals and exchanges, the result of what people have done for each other. For Fei the social person is born into and conceives itself as the result of rules of etiquette, of rites and rules of conduct that embed the social person in sets of highly differentiated roles. His conception can be described in terms of status and role, prescribed by rituals of social relations. They of course include rites of gift exchange and of the sharing of meals. But, unlike Strathern, Fei does not emphasize the substance and physical quality of ritual events and the experiencing body.

As a result of such studies as Strathern's, the study of kinship in the UK and North America turned away from models of prescribed conduct and systems of descent to studies of how in practice people in families and beyond families felt related to and indebted to others. 'Relatedness' was the name given to this theme. Janet Carsten edited a volume of such studies that was published in 2000, entitled *Cultures of Relatedness: New Approaches to the Study of Kinship*. These are studies not so much of how people are related to others according to rules of kinship, as studies of which relations matter, in a mixture of choice and rule. Choices are made about omitting some relations, maintaining or making others, and cutting off previously maintained relations. They are studies, not of given and prescribed relations but of the active maintenance of relations of kinship and other relations through exchanges of gifts, of visits, and the making and retaining of emotional bonds.

The biggest surprise to me, on reading Fei's *Xiangtu Zhongguo*, was how close *chaxugeju* is to this new approach to kinship. Again, as with Strathern, this book of Fei's was not known to Western anthropologists. Yet they, like *chaxugeju*, start from what used to be called kindred, those who are related to a social individual by both lines of descent and by marriage. Like *chaxugeju*, the anthropological conception of relatedness does not make a sharp distinction of family from lineage. Like *chaxugeju* and subsequent studies of affinity and friendship in Chinese social life, 'relatedness' stresses relations of reciprocity (*renqing*) and social affection (*ganqing*) (Bernard Gallin 1960, and Morton Fried 1953), pioneers in Western Chinese studies). But with this surprising similarity come some important differences.

These are best seen in contrast to the study of Chinese relatedness that is contained in Janet Carsten's book, which comes in the form of a study conducted by Charles Stafford in Taiwan. In it he shows how family reproduction, which is the main axis of Fei's concern, is not simply a matter of consanguinity, as it was for Fei. Having children and looking after parents is a reciprocal relationship of return for the nurturance (*yang*) provided by parents, and particularly by mothers, for their children. And the relations that are kept within a family, flexibly defined as it is for Fei, are similar to the relations that are made and maintained between families in reciprocal visits and gift exchanges (*laiwang*).

This element of choice seems to be missing from Fei's idea of consanguinity, and so is the importance of the mother. In general, the importance of women, both in the making and maintaining of relationships, and in the reciprocity of care for children and for the elderly, is missing. But the biggest difference concerns Western individualism and kinship. Instead of the close, small, and emotional family that Fei defined as a life fortress in his book on the American character, as he repeats in *Xiangtu Zhongguo* (p. 85), a large number of studies of UK and US kinship have shown how Western families are embedded in circles of association radiating from the social persons at their centres, just as in *chaxugeju* (see, for example, Wallman, 1984 *Eight London Families*). There is still a contrast to be made with agrarian Chinese and other kinship systems that have long genealogical records through which they trace origins in places other than those to which they presently belong and through which they can claim support and sometimes rights to a share in property. British and American kinship is generally shallower and is also much more cognatic, calculated through both lines of descent, through both mother and father. It therefore has the potential to include far more kin, so it requires, more often than in China, the omission of potential kin from relatedness. Most Western families calculate their genealogy to trace their roots and their sentimental sense of belonging, which is nearly always to more than one place of origin, or to trace their genetic medical history to forge a sense of identity over many generations rather than for any economic purpose, as was the case in agrarian China. British and American kinship are more like *chaxugeju*, but they are not the same. Similarly, we have to qualify the contrast with individualism by greater precision about where and how it exists.

Western individualism is far more a matter of laws of property, of Christian Protestant ethics, and of the disciplining of subjects to be self-regulating individuals than it is of the practising social person in association with other persons. So Fei's conclusions about the Western family and *tuantigeju* and Marilyn Strathern's much later contrast with Western individualism both have to be modified. Western individualism is a legal, an ethical and a disciplinary practice stressing individual self-regulation and individual property rights. It is lived out in relations of power and the ideologies of equality before the law and of public opinion as the source of governmental legitimacy, which in practice is dominated by mass media and the powers and financing of political persuasion through them. They do not describe actual sociality and social practice.

There remains some truth in Fei's observation that the nuclear family of parents and children in North America and the UK is a resort of emotional support, and that this is not at all the main function of a Chinese agrarian family. The economic, work and organizational, functions of a Chinese rural family were far more important than they were for an urban Western family. But this too has to be qualified. His model of the small family as the primordial unit of Western society, which he took from Western sociology, assumes that the nuclear family is the stable centre of social life. But this was a correct assumption for only a short historical period, one that lasted only a century and a half. The stable nuclear family was to be found in Europe only after the mid-nineteenth century, and has now become more like a series of nuclear families, with increasing rates of remarriage and the formation of a series of new sexual partnerships, linked through the care of children and by children maintaining relationships with both parents and step-parents. Accepting this qualification, it is still true that conjugal couples and their children are important for emotional support and for informal education in the ideology of self-regulation, and that this can be contrasted with the Chinese concentric circles of differential association through consanguinity with vital economic and not just emotional functions.

This observation about how right Fei was, once we add the necessary qualifications, brings us to another big question. What alterations have occurred in the family in China with the great economic changes and transformations in the organization of work since the 1940s? Has the emotional function become more important in Chinese family life, now that most people living in the Chinese countryside no longer depend on agricultural earnings?

The emotional family in China

Fei argued in *Xiangtu Zhongguo* that 'the force that stabilises social relationships is not emotion (*ganqing*) but understanding (*liaojie*)….accepting a common frame of reference' (p. 88). He contrasts what he calls the romantic Western quest for unity through love between the sexes as an adventure and an experiment with the rural Chinese acceptance of sexual differences and avoidance of emotionality in favour of fixed codes of conduct. Other students of Chinese society have shown that sexual and romantic love is kept for relationships separate from family. But this is not a distinction of *liaojie* from *ganqing*. It is a distinction between *qing* – which I would translate into English as 'affection' and which is learned and cultivated in family and friendship – and *lian'ai*, which is passionate love. I wonder whether Fei's separating of *ganqing* from *liaojie* is necessary, but I do accept his distinction from what he calls the Faustian adventure of romantic love. Like Fei, two Chinese American social psychologists, Francis Hsu and Godwin Chu, made their own contrasts with Western individualism and considered that romantic passion is absent from the Chinese social self based securely in its significant others of immediate kin (Hsu 1985: 35–41, Chu 1985: 264–267). To them, the promotion of romantic passion to the centre of social discourse and the arts in the West is based on the individual and autonomous self. But there have been tremendous changes since the 1940s in China.

William Jankowiak's study of the city of Huhehot in the 1980s and early 90s shows that young people now include in their criteria for their ideal mate not just practical, economic and instrumental values, but also the value of romantic passion as a life-enhancing experience. They have been combined in courtship; the romance and passion that had been separated from marriage is now part of it (1995: 182).

Yan Yunxiang's study (2003) of Xiajia, a village in Heilongjiang, traces the beginnings of individualism in children of both sexes to the great opening to all, male and female, of earning individual incomes in the form of work points in collective production. This has been accelerated by the far greater opportunities of earning cash incomes in separate occupations, jobs or enterprises. Yan notes that in Xiajia this has been accompanied by a process of breaking the taboo on pre-marital sex associated with romance. An engaged couple would go together to the city to buy their wedding goods and get photographed and they would stay overnight in town and sleep together, thus declaring that 'the rice is cooked'. Even on visits to future in-laws, now that houses had separate rooms, it had become possible by the 1990s for intending couples to sleep together before marriage. Moreover, brides themselves now negotiate their bridewealth, expressing indi-viduality and initiative by having their own earning capacity. One result is that couples insist on having their own domestic unit, in a separate building. Yan also notes that young women like fluency in words of love, including the lines of pop-song lyrics. All this romance and choice is still pre-*marital*; it is not casual sex. But it does point to the emergence, not just in urban but also in rural China, of something like Fei's American fortress family. Indeed, Yan Yunxiang's book has the title Private Life in Socialist China, and in it he argues that modernity is uni-versal, including individualism and the privacy of domestic life and its separation from work and economic life, and that it has come to Chinese rural society.

Conclusions

What conclusions can we draw from this extension of Fei's sustained comparison?

First of all, we can conclude that social egoism and the differential mode of association was, like individualism in the West, an ethic and a code of practice for social life. But it was governed by ritual, not by law, and it was cultivated and reproduced first in the family that was also a small lineage, taking consanguinity as the root of social reproduction and as the first priority of loyalty. That does not exclude the possibility that in rural society domestic life was emotional and ex-perienced in different ways with quite a lot of flexibility. Similarly, individualism is nurtured in Western family life, yet family life is experienced as a flexible and associative social life, governed by expectations and obligations in the same way as in China, though not the *same* expectations and obligations. Individualism is mainly cultivated outside the family, in school, in institutions of welfare and in political discourse and the family is not the first priority of loyalty, just one among others, although it is through family that a sense of belonging is traced to other places. In short, Fei's distinction holds true, but it must be seen as a contrast between ideologies and discourses prevailing in agrarian China and until now, and in the nineteenth-century West until now.

Secondly, we can ask whether social egoism and the differential mode of association have remained the same, whether roles and status differences have changed, and therefore whether the ideals and expectations of *renqing* and *ganqing* are governed by a fixed code, as Fei assumed they were. I would suggest that they were always more flexible than Fei assumed. They were in any case not just relations of consanguinity but also relations of affinity and friendship, expectations of trust and reciprocity in hierarchical relations. So, now that hierarchical relations of leadership, class and wealth have changed, so must the differential mode of association and the circles drawn by social egoists. Crucially, with the spread and tremendously increased importance of economic relations without human feelings (*wuqing*), surely the new mode of differential association has become something like a large fortress of affection (*qing*) and expectation of trust and the doing of public good among neighbours as well as friends and family. At the same time it has expanded as a way of doing business and forming political alliances. A number of recent studies confirm these suggestions. I refer in particular to Chang Xiangqun's work, in which all previous studies are considered together and applied to a close study of how interpersonal relations are calculated and how they have been both sustained and changed creatively in the village first studied by Fei.

From this and other studies, I think we can conclude that the differential mode of association is still a strong characteristic of Chinese society, but that it has changed and expanded considerably, as morally trustworthy relations are created and maintained across far greater expanses of social relationships, while forming a counterpoint to the even greater expansion of purely instrumental and anonymous economic relations.

Finally, let me turn again to the big political question raised by Fei. Can these relations of reciprocity and obligation become the basis for a local political life that checks the demands of a powerful central state, and, I would add, can it check the ruthlessness of a capitalist economy? In my opinion, we have to look in other directions within the traditions of Chinese society to add relations of locality and neighbourhood to consanguinity and the differential mode of association to begin to answer this question. It is also a question that cannot be answered without at the same time taking into account the fact that some of the mechanisms of elected representation and the ideals of individualism have been imported from the West and have been part of Chinese politics for more than a century. We must also add the fact that ideals of social justice in China have been mixed with those of socialism also imported from the West. Nevertheless, even after we have taken all this into consideration, looking at a rural China that is no longer chiefly agrarian, I think it is surprisingly still necessary and important to accept Fei's political project. Professor Fei's search for gradual reform, building modern Chinese institutions of economic and political organization on the basis of a transformed social egoism, is still a major project for practical research.

References

Carsten, Janet. ed. 2000. *Cultures of Relatedness: New Approaches to the Study of Kinship*. Cambridge, UK: Cambridge University Press.

— 2005. *After Kinship*. Cambridge, UK: Cambridge University Press.

Chang, Xiangqun. 2004. *Lishang-wanglai – social support networks, reciprocity and creativity in a Chinese village* (PhD thesis). City University, London

— 2010. *Guanxi or Li shang wanglai? Reciprocity, Social Support Networks, & Social Creativity in a Chinese Village*. Taipei: Scholarly Publishing Business, Airiti Press Inc.

Chu, Godwin C. 1985. 'The changing concept of self in contemporary China' in A. J. Marsella et al. eds. *Culture and Self: Asian and Western Perspectives*. Sydney: Law Book Co of Australasia, 252–278

Mary Douglas. 1970. *Natural Symbols: Explorations in Cosmology*. London: Routledge.

Fei, Hsiao-Tung. 1939. *Peasant Life in China: a field study of country life in the Yangtze valley*. London: Routledge & Kegan Paul LTD，1939 [费孝通：《江村经济：中国农民的生活》，南京：江苏人民出版社1986年版。]

— 1953. *China's Gentry: Essays in Rural-Urban Relations*. Edited and revised by Margaret Park Redfield Margaret Park Redfield. Chicago and London: University of Chicago.

费孝通：《乡土中国》，北京：三联书店，1948年版 [Xiangtu Zhongguo (From the soil), Beijing: SDX Joint Publishing Company. 1948].

— 乡土重建》，上海：上海观察社，1948年版 [Xiangtu Zhongguo (Reconstructing Rural China) Shanghai: Shanghai Guancha Publisher. 1948.]

— 美国人的性格》，上海：生活书店1947年版。[The American Character (Meiguoren de Xingge, Shanghai: Shenghuo, 1947)].

Fei, Hsiao-Tung and Chang, Chih. 1949. *Earthbound China: A Study of Rural Economy in Yunnan*. London: Routledge.

Feuchtwang, Stephan. 1992. *The Imperial Metaphor: Popular Religion in China*. London and New York: Routledge.

Fincher, John H. 1981. *Chinese Democracy: The Self-government Movement in Local, Provincial and National Politics, 1905–1914*. New York: St. Martin's Press.

Freedman, Maurice. 1961. 'Sociology in China: A brief survey' in G. William Skinner. ed. 1979. *The Study of Chinese Society* Stanford: Stanford University Press, 373–379.

— 1974. 'The politics of an old state' in G. William Skinner. ed. 1979. *The Study of Chinese Society*. Stanford: Stanford University Press, 334–350.

Fried, Morton H. 1953. The *Fabric of Chinese Society: A Study of the Social Life of a Chinese County Seat*. New York: Praeger.

Gallin, Bernard. 1960. 'Matrilineal and affinal relationships of a Taiwanese village', *American Anthropologist* 62(4): 632–642.

Hamilton, Gary G. and Wang Zheng. 1992. *From the Soil, The Foundations of Chinese Society: A translation of Fei Xiaotong's Xiangtu Zhongguo*. Berkeley, Los Angeles and London: University of California Press.

Hsu, Francis L.K. 1985. 'The self in cross-cultural perspective' in Marsella, Devos and Hsu. eds. *Culture and Self: Asian and Western perspectives*. New York: Tavistock Publications, 24–55.

Jankowiak, William. 1995. 'Romantic passion in the People's Republic of China' in his ed. *Romantic Passion: A Universal Experience?* New York: Columbia University Press, 166–183.

Marsella, Anthony J., DeVos, George, and Hsu, Francis L.K. eds. 1985. *Culture and Self; Asian and Western Perspectives*. New York and London: Tavistock Publications.

Nadel, S.F. 1951. *The Foundations of Social Anthropology*. Glencoe: Free Press.

Schneider, David M. (1980 [1968]) *American Kinship: A Cultural Account*. Chicago: University of Chicago Press.

Stafford, Charles. 2000. 'Chinese patriliny and the cycles of *yang* and *laiwang*' in Carsten ed. *Cultures of Relatedness: New Approaches to the Study of Kinship*, 41–47

Strathern, Marilyn. 1988. *The Gender of the Gift: Problems with Women and Problems with Society in Melanesia*. Berkeley: University of California Press.

Wallman, Sandra. 1984. *Eight London Households*. London and New York: Tavistock Publications.

Wang Mingming. 2002. 'The Third Eye: Towards a critique of "nativist anthropology"', *Critique of Anthropology* 22 (2): 149–174.

Yan Yunxiang. 2003. *Private Life Under Socialism: Love, Intimacy, and Family in a Chinese Village 1949–1999*. Stanford: Stanford University Press.

Zhao Bingxiang. 2004. '"The Place where the Sage wouldn't go" and "The Place where the Sage was born": Mutual definitions of place in Shandong and Heilongjiang' in Feuchtwang, Stephan. ed. *Making Place: State Projects, Globalisation and Local Responses in China*. London: UCL Press, 117–132.

DOI https://doi.org/10.24103/GCSS1.en.2015.7

Afterword

It has been five years since we organized the event entitled 'Understanding China and Engaging with Chinese People – Commemorating the 100th Anniversary of Professor Fei Xiaotong's Birth' at the London School of Economics and Political Science in 2010. Now that the first volume derived from the event is finally ready to see the light of day, I have mixed thoughts and feelings.

First, the change of title, from 'Understanding China and Engaging with Chinese People', which was the title of the event in 2010, to 'The Globalization of China Social Sciences', the title of the present book, signifies a shift in perspective: the former looks at China from the outside, whereas the latter is the opposite. This shift reflects recognition of the existence of Chinese social sciences, and examines them as a subject within the framework of global social sciences.

Second, while working in the UK over the past two decades, I have learnt that Chinese social sciences have hitherto been generally little known and held in rather low esteem. However, this view has changed gradually in recent years. On the one hand, the many memorials and tributes to Fei Xiaotong have generated a large amount of social scientific work. Among the milestones that were marked were the 60th anniversary of Fei's fieldwork in Kaixiangong village in Jiangsu in 1996, the 80th anniversary of Fei's fieldwork in Yao Mantian in Guangxi in 2015, Fei's 80th birthday in 1990 and the 100th or 105th anniversary of his birth in 2010 and 2015, respectively; and after the 10th anniversaries of Fei's death in 2015, there will be more to come the 20th and 30th anniversaries of his death, and so on. We can expect another harvest year in 2016, the 80th anniversary of Fei's fieldwork in Kaixiangong! On the other hand, in the West, Fei Xiaotong has been celebrated at LSE, his alma mater, by the founding of the MSc China in Comparative Perspective by Stephan Feuchtwang in 2006, followed by the setting up of the Fei Xiaotong Prize for the best dissertation. Moreover, Professor Feuchtwang's talk on Fei has been included in the series of talks celebrating the 120th anniversary of the Department of Anthropology at LSE in 2015.

Third, having produced the first two volumes, we realized that the original intention to publish just a single volume on Fei in the Understanding China and the World series was very conservative. The articles we know of and those that are constantly being discovered give us confidence that Fei's work will easily fill six or eight volumes. Former World Bank Chief Economist and Senior Vice-president, Development Economics, Justin Yifu Lin, has written that China's rapidly rising economy has benefited from 'late development advantage'; in just the same way, I think that Chinese social sciences also have the late development advantage.

Fourth, although the quantity of production in the Chinese social sciences is adequate, it is difficult to know how we can make a real contribution to social sciences in the world. In the section on 'the significance of inventing and developing Chinese social science vocabularies' in 'Transculturality and the Globalization of Chinese Social Sciences', I point out that some articles published here 'demonstrate, on the one hand, how Chinese scholars are producing innovative ideas on a normalized social scientific basis; and, on the other hand, how non-Chinese scholars are conducting in-depth studies on China by seeking to understand and re-evaluate Chinese scholars' work. Both Chinese and non-Chinese contributors are engaged in self-reflection in doing research on China, but are, at the same time, going beyond their own cultural limitations.' Stephan Feuchtwang himself well exemplifies how views on Fei's work are changing. This can be seen from his two articles in this book, which show the trajectory of the change.

Finally, I sincerely thank all the contributors for their patience and active cooperation, academic advisers' and experts' sharp criticism and valuable advice, the translators for their skilful work, and the copy editors, graphic designers, typesetters and proofreaders for the final touches they put to the volume.

Xiangqun Chang
London, 3rd November 2015

DOI https://doi.org/10.24103/GCSS1.en.2015.8.1

Appendix A
Chinese for Social Sciences

Bridge & Artificial Limb
桥梁与假肢

宣力 (Lik Suen) 编[1]

著名社会学家费孝通在他的著作《乡土中国》中提出,"文化靠记忆传承。因此词是最重要的桥梁。"这些词语表达就像桥梁一样,存在于几代人之间。老一辈的中国人和年青一代中国人,因为有语言这个桥梁可以交流,所以文化得到延续。

汉学研究的是中国文化,所以离不开观察中文,借助汉语的词汇。可是,语言会有词不达意的时候,儿童文学作品《小王子中》有一句话说:"语言是误解的源泉。"("Language is the source of misunderstandings"),表达的就是这个意思。而跨文化翻译的局限更大,造成的误解也更多。英文中也有一个表达,"Lost in translation" 说的是翻译造成的错觉,以及翻译在文化面前的无能为力。

汉学家胜雅律先生关心中文中的概念和语言,在翻译成外文的过程中是如何受到影响的。他详细地比较了中文 "谋略"一词在英文文献中的各种翻译,认为把"谋略"翻译为"战略",只是抓住了词义的一个侧面,没有将真实意义解释清楚,因而形成文化上的错觉。

胜雅律先生认为语言及其表达的概念在跨文化交际中,要保持本土化。他强调翻译中要克服'编码眼光',不能简单地进行词与词的直接转换,而是要深入理解中国的文化历史和中国人的思维方式,去寻找准确的翻译。只有这样,语言才能成为跨文化交流中的桥梁,而不是似是而非,功能有限的 "假肢"。

标签: 社科汉语　　级别: 中级　　字数: 506

---

[1] 本文是作者根据发表在本刊的胜雅律 (Harro von Senger) 的原作:《谋略 (Supra-planning): 关于在中西方文化交流语境下翻译本土词汇及其概念的理解问题》一文, 节选、改编并改写为社科汉语的中级读物。感谢广州大学中文系王凤霞教授在伦敦大学亚非学院访问期间对本文的帮助, 同时谢谢全球中国比较研究会的志愿研究、翻译和编辑人员的积极参与, 他们是: 中国重庆大学法学院博士候选人杨宇静、香港理工大学中国语言文学专业硕士研究生王思齐、以及双语系本科生王冰然和武潇潇。

生词

桥梁	qiáoliáng	bridge
假肢	jǐazh-ı	artificial limb
著作	zhùzuò	book
靠	kào	by; rely on
记忆	jìyì	memory
传承	chuánchéng	inheritance
存在	cúnzài	exist
辈	bèi	generation
代	dài	generation, era
交流	ji-aoliú	exchange
延续	yánxù	continue; the continuation of
观察	gu-anchá	observation
借助	jièzhù	with the help of
误解	wùjǐe	misunderstanding
源泉	yuánquán	source
表达	bǐaodá	expression
跨文化	kuà wénhuà	intercultural; cross cultural
翻译	f-anyì	translate, translation
局限	júxiàn	limit; limited
错觉	cuòjué	illusion
概念	gàiniàn	concept
详细	xiángxì	detailed
谋略	móulüè	strategy
战略	zhànlüè	strategy
抓住	zhu-a zhù	catch; grasp
侧面	cèmiàn	side
真实	zh-enshí	true
因而	y-ın'ér	thus
形成	xíngchéng	form
交际	ji-aojì	communication
本土化	bǐentǔ huà	localization
克服	kèfú	overcome
编码	bi-anmǎ	code; coding
眼光	yǐangu-ang	vision
直接	zhíji-e	direct
转换	zhuǎnhuàn	change; transformation
深入	sh-enrù	thorough; in-depth
思维	s-ıwéi	thinking
方式	f-angshì	mode; method
准确	zhǐunquè	accurate

功能	g-ongnéng	function
有限	yˇouxiàn	limited

短语

词不达意:	Cí bù dá yì	(The language fails to express the meaning)
无能为力:	Wú néng wéi lì	(powerless; incapable of action)
似是而非:	Sì shì ér f-ei	(appear / look right, but in fact wrong)
受到影响:	Shòudào yˇıngxiˇang	(to be affected)

思考题

1) 文章中的"桥梁"与"假肢"指的是什么？
2) "语言是误解的源泉。"你同意这个说法吗？可以举几个例子吗？
3) 胜雅律先生说的'编码眼光'是什么意思？

详细阅读：

请参考本期胜雅律原文：《谋略(supraplanning)——中西文化交流中本土词汇与概念转换的问题》

DOI https://doi.org/10.24103/GCSS1.en.2015.8.2

Interpretation of China's Policies and Regulations with Thirty-Six Stratagems
用"三十六计"解读中国的政策法规[1]

宋连谊 编

语言不仅是过去与现在、同一文化下代际之间的桥梁，更是不同文化的人们之间的桥梁。本文聚焦于中西文化交流，即在讲述文化之间语言及语言所带来的概念的转换。

本土的语言和概念能够被转译为另一种文化吗？这种转译方法能够使其在另一种文化环境中被理解甚至实践，而同时保持它的本土性？

什么是"本土词汇"？即是那些在外文词语中很难找到能与之准确对应的词汇。面对这样的词语，人们经常用一种简单的方法，即选择一种便捷的翻译方式，用一个已经存在的、表面看来似乎对应的外语词汇去套，因此，就往往错过了"本土词汇"的真正意义。

在此，我以中文的"谋略"这一深深的扎根于古代和现代中国的规划艺术 (Art of Planning) 的词汇为例。

就这个"神秘"的中国词汇"谋略"而言，那些中国作者在试图将"谋略"翻译成英语语汇时却简单地使用了诸如"策略"或"战略"等术语。在西方，中文术语"谋略"至今仍未受到学术界的关注。在美国的出版物中，少有的几位专家把"谋略" 译成英语 (Detweiler 2010: 9, 13-15)。

一些中国和美国的作者或机构太过简单的使用诸如"战略欺骗" (strategic deception)、"计谋" (stratagem)、"战略与计谋" (strategy and stratagems) 或"战略 (strategy)"，作为"谋略"的表达方式。

"谋略"是什么意思？就专业意义而言，它有着相当特殊的含义，而西方本土语言中是没有合适的术语来描绘的。除非在西方语言中创造出一个新的表达法。

理解谋略含义最关键的一点是"谋略"高于"战略"，也就是说"谋略"在规划中位于战略之上 （拉丁文为*supra*），而在西方最高的规划水平是战略。我不认为西方在规划方面存在高于战略规划水平的词汇。

《孙子兵法》最高的境界是"不战而屈人之兵"，通常解释为"不通过战争来征服敌人" (Jullien 1996: 63)。

---

[1] 本文是作者根据发表在本刊的胜雅律 (Harro von Senger) 的原作：《谋略 (Supra-planning): 关于在中西方文化交流语境下翻译本土词汇及其概念的理解问题》一文，节选、改编并改写为社科汉语的高级读物。感谢南昌大学外语学院、剑桥大学访问学者徐海燕副教授对本文的帮助，同时谢谢全球中国比较研究会的志愿研究、翻译和编辑人愿的积极参与，他们是：上海应用技术学院社会工作系副教授刘群博士、英国谢菲尔德大学东亚研究系博士候选人郭成倩，以及香港理工大学翻译专业硕士研究生王思菡。

据我所知，尽管这里写"人"，而非"敌"，所有西方翻译家和西化了的华人翻译家对这句话的翻译都与这个句子的原意有所偏离，将其翻译为"敌"。

基于这个对"人"的解释，我对这个句子的翻译如下：

Without using arms to subdue the army of the **men** of the other side is the best.

通过这个翻译可见，这句话不是着眼于"敌"字上，而是将"人"凸显出来了。这样，较之于很多西方人和西化的中国人的翻译，这个句子就获得了新的以及更长时段的维度。这个例子表明了对自身本土性和对中国本土思维认识的重要性。

顺便提及，在我们眼皮下"不战而屈人之兵善之善者也"难道不正在被中华人民共和国使用吗？比如她并未把台湾视作一个"敌人"，多年以来通过越来越紧密的经济关系，使台湾人的"独立"越来越不可能，这是一种如"熊猫爪子"般轻柔，又不引人注意的和平统一的做法。

由于"战略"或"大战略"(grand strategy)不适合中国传统军事思维中的极度"长时段"(Jullien, 1996: 101)的预测视野，因而我建议不用已有的西方术语来描述《孙子兵法》中的规划的艺术，而是用中文词语"谋略"。但"谋略"应该如何翻译以保持其本土性？由于中国谋略高于(拉丁文为*supra*) 西方的战略，因此我选用"supraplanning"这个词作为"谋略"的英文翻译。

中国的谋略实践

1979年7月1日颁布的《中华人民共和国中外合资经营企业法》第5条规定：

> 合营企业各方可以现金、实物、工业产权等进行 投资。外国合营者作为投资的技术和设备，必须确实是适合我国需要的先进技术和设备。如果有意以落后的技术和设备进行欺骗，造成损失的，应赔偿损失。

以谋略之眼光来看，你很快就会意识到在这一法规中，至少三十六计中的两个计谋都在其中，第十九条"釜底抽薪"和第三十条"反客为主"。中华人民共和国以合资的法律形式将先进的技术从西方企业中吸取出来的策略(釜底抽薪)，从而达到反客为主的目的，即从一个依靠外国技术的国家变成一个有自己技术的国家。从谋略的角度来说，即便是在阅读法律文本时也应该随时铭记于心，很可能有某些计谋隐藏其中。

理查德·尼克松在北京大学的一次演讲中说：

> 有这样一种说法，美国人思考几十年的事......但是中国人思考几个世纪的事。(英帆 1988: p. 210 f.)

而阿尔·戈尔在他的《重塑美国力量的时代挑战》(2008年7月17日)的演讲报告中讲到：

> 十年是我们这个民族能建立并完成目标的最长期限。(Gore, 2008)

也就是说最主要的西方国家的战略规划水平最长也不过是10年。在中国则完全不同，邓小平在1992年的南巡过程中曾这样说过：

> 坚持党的基本路线，一百年不动摇。

在2012年11　月14日《中国共产党章程》重申了这样的阐述(在以往的章程如2002年和2007年的章程中也有相关阐述)：

> 我国正处于并将长期处于这会主义初级阶段。这是在经济落后的中国建设社会主义现代化不可逾越的历史阶段，需要上百年的时间。

此外，在上述《中国共产党章程》中，均设定了两个百年目标(俗称百年大计)：

> 在新世纪新阶段，经济和社会发展的战略目标是，巩固和发展已经初步达到的小康水平，到建党一百年时　(2021年)，建成惠及十几亿人口的更高水平的小康社会；到建国一百年时(2049年)，人均国内生产总值达到中等发达国家水平，基本实现现代化。

这两个100年的目标已经被载入以前的章程中，如2002和2007年。正如20世纪80年代中早期，中共主席胡耀邦曾预测，为了富国强民，中华人民共和国将要在21世纪的头30至50年间努力奋斗(von Senger 1985b)。

中国的寓言故事"愚公移山"更加表明中国规划周期比美国的最长规划的周期还要长得多。

中国的政治谋略对西方商人来说也意味深长。这里我要讲的一点是中国直至2021年和2049年的长期规划。在这样长的时间周期里，中国需要与国外商业保持联系，不然它将不能突破"长期"的"社会主义初级阶段"的落后局面，这对于西方商人来说意味着一种高度的规划上的保障。另一方面，西方人不应该忽视"谋略"的第二个方面，而应熟知中国的智谋学。如果没有这些知识，他们是无法与中国商业伙伴的智谋相匹敌的。

纵使中文词汇再有本土性，也并不意味着一定要造许多新词。其实，发现恰当的西方词汇能成为翻译中文词汇的优秀"桥梁"。例如，中文"三十六计"中的"计"，就能很好的由"stratagem"来表达，这源于古希腊词汇"strategema"，在现代西方英语中又有两个意义1) 军事计谋2) 普通意义上的计谋。(von Senger, 1991: 1 ff.)

创造一个新的西方词汇来翻译"谋略"有什么用呢？

首先，通过这个新词，希望普通的西方人能够知道中国有自己的词汇和概念。

- 以英语和德语为例，在面对复杂的世界它们有时太过于本土和狭窄。
- 以他们本土语言的词汇为基础，他们并不了解外国文化遗产中的所有的细微差别。
- "Supraplanning"这个新的词可能会对西方人产生一点点冲击，因为如果不向他们解释，他们就不知道这词意味着什么。这种冲击哪怕只是一点点，也就达到了我期望这个词所产生的效果。

词汇

代际	dài jì	intergenerational
便捷	biànjié	convenient
套	tào	to fit something into a frame
扎根	zhágēn	rooted
诸如	zhūrú	such as
术语	shùyǔ	terminology
偏离	piānlí	deviate
凸显	tūxiǎn	highlight
维度	wéidù	dimension
产权	chǎnquán	property
眼皮	yǎnpí	the eyelids
赔偿	péicháng	compensation
铭记	míngjì	always remember
重塑	chóng sù	remodeling
南巡	nán xún	inspection tour of the South
阐述	chǎnshù	elaborate
章程	zhāngchéng	constitution
小康	xiǎokāng	fairly well-off
惠及	huìjí	to benefit
寓言	yùyán	fable
智谋	zhìmóu	resourcefulness
匹敌	pǐdí	rival
纵使	zòngshǐ	even though
釜底抽薪	fǔ dǐ chōu xīn	(take away the firewood from under the cauldron; drastic; a fundamental solution)
反客为主	fǎn kè wéi zhǔ	(turn from a guest into a host)
铭记于心	míng jì yú xīn	(keep in mind)
隐藏其中	yǐn cáng qí zhōng	(hidden among)
不可逾越	bù kě yú yuè	(insurmountable, impassable)
愚公移山	Yú gōng yí shān	(Foolish Old Man removed the mountains; the determination to win victory and the courage to surmount every difficulty)
孙子兵法	Sūnzǐ bīng fǎ	(Sun Tzu's Art of War; Sun Zi's Art of War)
三十六计	sān shí liù jì	(Thirty-Six Stratagems)

练习1 词语学习 - 将下列词语译成英文:

政策法规	代际之间	概念转换	据我所知
凸显出来	法律文本	相关阐述	设定目标
百年大计	初步达到	富国强民	努力奋斗
意味深长	商业伙伴	文化遗产	细微差别

练习2 讨论题

1) 你如何理解并翻译下列词语？他们有什么区别？
   计战略   计谋 策略 战术 谋略
2) 谈谈你对'谋略'的理解，并试着选用生活、战争、商业、政策、法规等方面中的例子加以说明。

DOI https://doi.org/10.24103/GCSS1.en.2015.8.3

Ripples and Straws
水圈和干草

宣力 (Lik Suen) 编[1]

　　费孝通是二十世纪中国最有影响力的社会科学家。他只发表了几部英语著作,他的晚年绝大部分关于中国社会的著作都是用中文出版的，因此，他的思想在西方社会科学界没有什么影响。近年来,他的研究越来越受到西方汉学家和社会科学家的关注,甚至认为他的研究为西方理解中国指明了一条道路。

　　费孝通最有名的著作是《乡土中国》，写于1947年。在这本书中他对中西方社会做了对比，认为中西方社会差异巨大，而差异的核心是"世界观"的不同。费孝通说中国的社会关系是水圈,而西方的社会关系是干草。水圈是说,从社会关系上来看,每个人都在他特定的社会关系网络的中心。最亲近的关系是家庭,包括父亲、母亲、兄弟和姐妹。基于各自的角色，每个人都有义务遵从地位高的人。每一对关系都是不同的,而且每个人服从的行为也是有差异的。当家庭关系向外扩展到邻居、同学、工作中的同事时,就会产生新的关系。在亲近关系圈内，服从是必须的；但在较远的关系圈内，有余地去选择是否服从。从自我出发,建立一个亲友关系网络,在这个网络中,每个人都是关联的，彼此之间存在责任和义务。费孝通认为这就是中国人世界观，并影响着他们的一生。费孝通认为西方社会像是一个由稻草堆成的干草堆。每一根稻草是独立且平等的。一根根稻草组成了一束束干草，然后形成干草捆，最后,所有的干草捆放在一起便成了干草堆。费孝通过这个比喻,说明西方社会中的个体是独立平等的，他们属于一个组织，通过组织,个体可以获得权利与义务。

标签：社科汉语　　级别：中级　　字数：600

生词

费孝通	Fèi Xiàotōng	Chinese sociologist and anthropologist
世纪	shìjì	century
影响力	yǐngxiǎnglì	influence
内容	nèiróng	content
指明	zhǐmíng	show clearly, point out, demonstrate
差异	chāyì	difference, diversity
巨大	jùdà	huge, enormous, gigantic

---

[1]　本文是作者根据发表在本刊的韩格理 (Gary G. Hamilton) 的原作:《费孝通著作对西方社会科学家的启示》一文，节选、改编并改写为社科汉语的中级读物。

核心	héxīn	nucleus, core, key
水圈	shuǐquān	hydrosphere
干草	gāncǎo	hay; dried millet stalks
特定	tèdìng	specified
网络	wǎng luò	networks
亲近	qīnjìn	be intimate with, be friends with
基于	jīyú	in view of, because of
各自	gèzì	each one; respective
角色	juésè	role, part (in a play, etc)
义务	yìwù	duty, obligation
遵从	zūncóng	comply with, follow
服从	fúcóng	obey, follow, submit to
扩展	kuòzhǎn	expand, extend, spread, develop
邻居	línjū	neighbour
有余地	yǒuyúdì	(have) flexibility
是否	shìfǒu	whether or not; is it (or not)
自我	zìwǒ	oneself; self-
关联	guānlián	be related, be connected
彼此	bǐcǐ	each other
责任	zérèn	responsibility, duty; accountability
稻草	dàocǎo	rice straw
独立	dúlì	independent
平等	píngděng	equal; equality
束	shù	tie, bind, bundle
干草捆	gāncǎokǔn	bale of hay
比喻	bǐyù	draw an analogy; analogy, metaphor
属于	shǔyú	belong to
权利	quánlì	right

短语

乡土中国	xiāng tǔ zhōng guó (rural China; *From the Soil*)
社会关系	shehui guanxi (social relationships)

思考题

1. 请简单介绍一下费孝通。
2. 如何理解中国人的社会关系是"水圈"?
3. 费孝通认为西方社会关系像干草堆,你同意这种比喻吗?

详细阅读

请参考本期韩格理原文:《费孝通著作对西方社会科学家的启示》

DOI https://doi.org/10.24103/GCSS1.en.2015.8.4

A Chinese Map and a Raphael Fresco
中国地图与拉斐尔的壁画

宋连谊 (Lianyi Song) 编[1]

费孝通是中国二十世纪最有影响力的社会科学家。那些致力于研究中国社会的学者认为费孝通的著作为构建一门研究中国社会、以中国为中心的社会学学科做出了非常重要的贡献。

费孝通于1947年试图通过《乡土中国》这本书来告知中国读者：中西方社会差异较大，且这并非表面现象，而是深入这两个社会最核心意义的范式或世界观。费孝通自创了一个关于中国社会组织架构的理想类型的概念，即"差序格局"，来描述中国人的世界观。费孝通用池塘里从内向外辐射的波纹作为类比来进一步解释"差序格局"，距离中心点越近，其影响越大于从中心点越走越远的波纹。

波纹意指社会关系，每个人都是在他/她特定的社会关系网络的中心点。与你最亲近的关系即家庭成员：父亲、母亲、兄弟、姐妹。依据各自的角色，每个人都有义务遵从地位更高的人。当从核心家庭关系向外扩展至邻居、同学、同乡、同事，这些角色也将带来不同的责任义务关系。费孝通认为，中国人生活在这社会世界中，这种世界观影响着他们的一生。

费孝通把与中国的"差序格局"相对的西方社会的世界观的称为"团体格局"。他认为西方社会更像是一个由一根根的稻草堆成的干草堆。每一根稻草是与他人不同且平等的。一根根稻草组成了一束束干草捆，干草捆聚堆成大的干草捆，所有的干草捆放在一起便成了干草堆。通过这个类比，费孝通意图说明西方社会中的个体是独立且平等的，他们从属于具有清晰界限的组织，个体通过组织可以在权利与义务上获得自我感。在每一个层次的组织中，个体的行为受到制约，权利与义务受到组织层次的限制，只要不侵犯其他人的权利和义务，他们有自由去做自己想做之事。

事实上这种类比所描述的意象在中西方社会里非常普遍。

水圈中的层层波纹在中国社会中是一个反复出现的意象，比如精雕细琢的一个套一个的象牙球。这种层层嵌套的雕琢方式有其哲学含义，它暗示了中国人的世界秩序观，最里最深的领域是家庭，最外侧的是天下，二者都在天之下。这种含义我们从早期中国的地图中可以更清晰的看出。图一是中国十五世纪的地图，中国的位置在图纸的正中心，其他国家围绕其外侧，有些距离远，有些距离近。这是一张反映了中国人的世界观的对已知世界的描绘，能从中窥见"中国的朝贡体系"，一个圈在一个圈之内。这张地图绝对无法为你从一国到他国导航，但是你能通过这张地图去看各国之间的关系，如韩国距离天朝很近，其他国家便很远。

---

[1] 本文是作者根据发表在本刊的韩格理 (Gary G. Hamilton) 的原作:《费孝通著作对西方社会科学家的启示》一文，节选、改编并改写为社科汉语的高级读物。

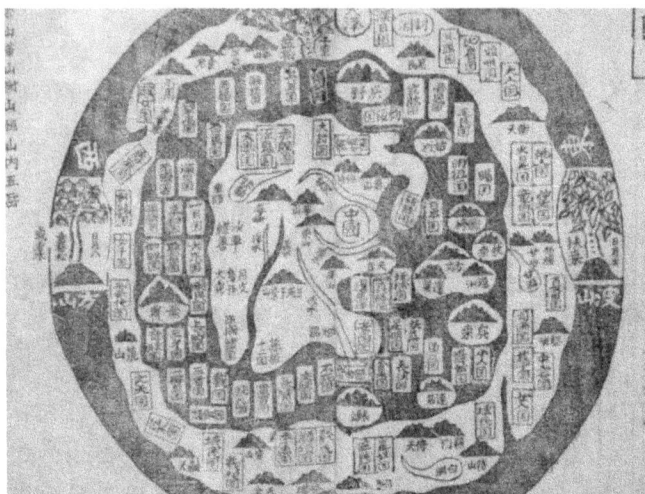

图一：十五世纪的中国地图，显示中国的朝贡关系

　　现在让我们看看费孝通使用的西方社会构成的意象：根根稻草成束再成捆，最后成了草堆。这种意象在西方社会是普遍存在的，从描绘各种现代组织的权力结构的简单图表中便显而易见。甚至在更早之前，早在这种描绘现代组织的方式流行之前，相同的组织意象也很普遍。图二便展示了这种意象的含意。这是一幅拉斐尔创作的壁画，简称"争议"(Disputa)，是在梵蒂冈教皇私人书房里发现的。从这幅画中我们可以看出十六世纪早期基督教界的等级制度：上帝端坐在最顶端手握着地球，周围环绕着天主，上帝看着我们，统领世界；基督在第二层的最中间，两侧是圣母玛利亚和施洗者约翰，周围环绕着先知和不同学科的人；位于最底层的是教皇、皇帝、红衣主教和其他世俗权威。他们争论话题是圣礼的意义。

图二：拉斐尔关于圣礼的纷争

在这幅壁画和那张描绘权力结构的图里，组织中的每一个人都屈从于处于最高的权威（或上帝），其权威超越了组织本身。图中掌握权威的人(或神) 的位置从中心向外辐射，更重要的是，权力被疏导到一个外显的结构中去。

费孝通提出的两种典型的社会模式展示了中西方社会里个体生存的差异。"差序格局"和"团体格局"都包括了等级的和横向的元素，但是两者的鲜明对比在于各自社会的秩序，这两种秩序是截然不同的。由于各自社会中的组织框架以不同的方式创造出他们各自的社会存在，因此中西方社会完全展示出两种不同的状态。

建议和扩展阅读

1. 中级社科汉语读物《水圈和干草 》(Ripples and straws)
2. 韩格理（Gary G. Hamilton）"费孝通著作对西方社会科学家的启示"原文

词组和成语

壁画	bìhuà	mural; wall painting
致力	zhìlì	to be devoted to
构建	gòujiàn	build; construction
贡献	gòngxiàn	contribution
试图	shìtú	to try, to attempt
差异	chāyì	difference
核心	héxīn	core
范式	fànshì	paradigm
架构	jiàgòu	framework
波纹	bōwén	ripple
意指	yì zhǐ	means
依据	yījù	basis
义务	yìwù	obligation
遵从	zūncóng	compliance
稻草	dàocǎo	straw
捆	kǔn	bundle
聚	jù	gather
堆	duī	heap
清晰	qīngxī	clear
制约	zhìyuē	restrict; control
侵犯	qīnfàn	invasion, violation
意象	yìxiàng	image, imagery
反复	fǎnfù	repeatedly
象牙	xiàngyá	ivory
嵌套	qiàn tào	nested
雕琢	diāozhuó	carve

领域	lǐngyù	area, field
外侧	wàicè	outside
含义	hányì	meaning
图纸	túzhǐ	drawing
围绕	wéirào	around; to surround
窥见	kuǐjiàn	peek; a glimpse of
朝贡	cháogòng	tribute; pay tribute
绝对	juéduì	absolutely
导航	dǎohán	navigation
天朝	tiāncháo	the Imperial China
展示	zhǎnshì	to show, to reveal
梵蒂冈	fàndìgāng	the Vatican
教皇	jiàohuáng	pope
上帝	shàngdì	God
端坐	duān zuò	sit up straight
顶端	dǐngduān	top (end)
握	wò	grip, hold
环绕	huánrào	surround
天主	tiānzhǔ	God
统领	tǒnglǐng	guide; command
基督	jīdū	Christ
施洗	shī xǐ	baptist
约翰	yuēhàn	John
主教	zhǔjiào	bishop
世俗	shìsú	secular
圣礼	shèng lǐ	sacraments
屈从	qūcóng	succumb to
辐射	fúshè	radiation
外显	wài xiǎn	explicit
秩序	zhìxù	order
框架	kuàngjià	frame
拉斐尔	Lāfěi'ěr	Raphael
圣母玛利亚	shèngwǔ Mǎlìyà	Virgin Mary
差序格局	differential mode of association	
团体格局	organizational mode of association	
精雕细琢	with the care and precision of a sculptor	
显而易见	obviously	
截然不同	completely different	

练习

1.   词语学习 （宗教词语）

教皇　上帝　天主　基督　施洗　主教
世俗　圣礼　圣母　圣母玛利亚　梵蒂冈

2.   用3-5句话(口语或书面)描述课文中的两幅插图
(图1: 十五世纪的中国地图, 图2: 拉斐尔关于圣礼的纷争)

3.   讨论或作文
1).   请你介绍一下费孝通对中西方社会典型模式的两个比喻 （即水圈和草垛）。
2).   你是否能用其他的比喻来描述中西方社会典型模式?
3).   韩格理 (Gary G. Hamilton) 在他的文章中例举了一些例子来说明费孝通的两个比喻。你是否能举出一些例子来说明这两个比喻?

DOI https://doi.org/10.24103/GCSS1.en.2015.8.5

English-Chinese Translation in Social Sciences
1. 社会科学中的英译汉问题

宋连谊 (Lianyi Song)

在本期的社科汉语的翻译栏目中，我们结合在本期发表的书评[1]选择介绍三个方面的问题：方言/外来语，社科词汇/词组/短语和翻译难句。

一、方言/外来语(dialect / loan words)

因所选文章涉及饮食，我们就从中选出几个跟饮食相关的词语加以介绍。

- *yum cha / yum-cha / yumcha* [广东话] 饮茶, (in Cantonese Chinese literally means 'drink tea')我们知道"饮"在普通话里就是"喝"的意思，"饮茶"就是"喝茶"。但是"饮"在普通话里只用于一些固定词语或习惯用语里，如: 饮料(drinks)、饮水机(water dispenser)、饮水思源(When one drinks water, one must not forget where it comes from; grateful)。类似的例子还有，在广东话里，食、话、行分别是普通话里的吃、说、走，等。学者考证认为这是因为广东话里仍保留着古汉语中的这些词的动词用法。
- *dim sum* [广东话] 点心(a style of Cantonese bite-sized food served in small steamer baskets or plates).
- *ramen* [日文] 日本拉面(a Japanese noodle soup dish served in a meat or fish-based broth with different flavoured material)
- *tempura* [日文]: 裹上淀粉或面粉浆油炸的海产或蔬(a Japanese dish of seafood or vegetables that have been battered and deep fried)。在日文中，*tempura*的汉字写法是"天麸羅"或"天婦羅"。中文的简繁体字分别写作天麸罗/天麸羅或天妇罗/天婦羅，以天妇罗/天婦羅更为常见。

二、社科词汇/词组/短语(phrases/glossaries)

每个专业都有其特定的词语或表述方式，社会科学领域则更是有许多专业术语。下面是我们从文章中选出几个例子。

---

1. 基于本期发表的陈奕麟撰写的书评: 《中餐的全球化》吴燕和、张展鸿(合编)檀香山: 夏威夷大学出版社，2002年, 216页(*The Globalization of Chinese Food*. Edited by David Y.H. Wu and Sidney C..H. Cheung. Honolulu, HI: University of Hawaii Press, 2002. 216pp)，全球中国比较研究会的志愿研究和翻译人员张昕博士(中国山西省电力行业协会高级经济师及资讯经理)和裴可诗女士(Costanza Pernigotti 全球中国比较研究会和中国浙江传媒学院研究人员)，在翻译此书评过程中整理出了基本素材，由已故全球中国比较研究会行政经理和执行编辑余小菠最后编校，在此一并致谢。

- an internally bound entity 一种内部绑定的实体
- intercultural influences / intercultural relations
  跨文化影响/跨文化关系
- markers and breakers of cultural barriers
  文化藩篱的标识者和破冰者
- ethnic identity 族群认同；民族认同
- 'Cuisines' are constructed tastes "佳肴"是人为建构的口味
- manifestations of class 阶级的表现；(社会)阶层的体现
- cultural authenticity 文化的真伪；文化的真实性
- everyday social interaction 日常生活社会互动
- institutionalized (even class) practices 制度化(甚至阶级)的做法；约
  定俗成(甚至体现社会阶层)的做法

从上面的译文中我们可以看到，一些词语可能会有不同的中文译文。我们在做翻译时，常常遇到字面意思和引申意义之间的差异，这是因为一些词语在没有上下文(context)的情形中，可能会是一个或多个意思，但是在具体的语境中，其意思则可能较为具体，可能不是通常字面呈现的意思。

在以上的几个词句中，我们选出几个略加深入探讨。

Class可以是"阶级"的意思，但也可以是"阶层"或"等级"的意思。说到饮食习惯，我们会听到或看到社会调查中提及：middle class(中产阶级)家庭的饮食习惯呈现某种特点等。我们也知道社会可以分为不同的阶层，而不一定是阶级。因此，manifestations of class 可以被译为"阶级的表现"，也可译为"(社会)阶层的体现"。

同样institutionalized (even class) practices 的译文可以按字面译为"制度化(甚至阶级)的做法"。这里，"制度化的做法"尚且可以接受，但说"阶级的做法"似不太符合习惯用法。我们可以考虑译为"约定俗成(甚至体现社会阶层)的做法"。

再举一例。"Cuisines" are constructed tastes. 我们知道 cuisine 可以有多种意思：菜系、菜肴、美食、烹饪等。但在这篇文章中，cuisine 不仅用了复数，而且放在了括号里，那么根据上下文，"佳肴"可能是个比较好的译文，因为这里谈的是某种 cuisine 可能是一种供"他人"消费而人为制造出来的味道。至于 construct/constructed 一词，可以译为"构建/构建的"。但什么是"人为构建的口味"呢？对普通的中文读者也许并不清楚。然而，"构建"一词所表达的概念似乎越来越被人们接受。也许随着"构建"一词的广泛使用，"构建的口味"将是普遍接受的表述。

三、翻译难句(difficult sentences)

我们在此挑选了几句我们认为在这篇书评的翻译中较费心思的译文。读者不妨先试着译一下下面的句子，然后再看参考译文，对参考译文加以评判，思考一下如何可以翻译得更准确和更得体。请注意，以下参考译文仅供参考，并不是完美的译法。

1) As historians, Dai and Ismail steer relatively clear of culture, given the explicit intercultural relations.
2) Their analyses seem to suggest a more subtle and significant relevance of social and institutional factors that neither would overtly admit.
3) The difference between food and cuisine is largely one between taste as literal meaning and institutional phenomenon.
4) Some are clear fabrications; some others have evolved and become institutions in their own right, to a point where beef noodles are now re-exported to Beijing as "Taiwanese" beef noodles.

参考中文译文如下：
1) 作为历史学家，戴一峰和伊斯梅尔都因为不同的文化之间有着明显的关联而在某种程度上回避了"文化"这个概念。
2) 他们分析的结果似乎表明社会因素和制度因素与饮食之间有着不可忽视的细微相关性，但两者都未明确地承认这一点。
3) 饭菜与菜系之间的区别主要在于一般意义上的"味道"与既定文化现象之间的不同。
4) 事实上，有些菜肴显然是新产品，有些却已经由原有菜肴演变为自成一家的食品，比如从台湾重新引进到北京的牛肉面被称为"台湾"牛肉面。

如你在翻译中有什么意见或心得，请告诉我们。建议将上述译法与该书评译者的译法之异同，思考一下是什么原因导致了社会科学工作者与专业翻译对同一文本的不同译法。

在结束本专栏的时候，我想总结两点。一是社科汉语的一些词语，特别是从英文或其他语言翻译成汉语时使用的一些汉语，可能不是我们生活中常用或熟悉的词义或用法。第二，英文中也有许多不同作者/学者创造出来的新词、概念和与众不同的表达方式，而这些常常没有现成的或自然贴切的汉语词语表达，或许译者会有意识地去反映原文的独特表述，译文中难免有一些生涩或别扭的词语和句子。也许一些"勉为其难"的中文译文会被修正，而有些也许就"一回生，二回熟"被人们接受了。我相信，在不断的交流和探讨过程中，中文在应对与世界交流和沟通的需求方面一定有强大的生命力。

DOI https://doi.org/10.24103/GCSS1.en.2015.8.6

Translation of Philosophy and Philosophy of Translation: Social Science Translation
哲学的翻译和翻译的哲学
谈社会科学中的英汉翻译的问题

冯东宁 (Dongning Feng)

本期的两篇书评向读者展现了纳维尔的《礼仪与敬意：在比较的语境中延伸中国哲学》和钟鸣旦的《礼仪的交织:明末清初中欧文化交流中的丧葬礼》的要旨和评价，因此便涉及到中国哲学思想和西方宗教文本的翻译。虽然儒学和宗教的翻译渊源已久，然而无论是在翻译理论还是翻译实践中有待探讨的问题，不仅没有因为全球化而减弱，而且问题更加深入化和多样化。在此我们就本刊书评的翻译来探讨以下几个方面的问题：哲学性概念的翻译，术语的翻译，以及结合复杂句谈谈自译的问题。

一、概念的翻译(translation of philosophical concepts)

"Confucius says"(孔子曰)已成为英语中表达智慧的前置用语，虽然这一用法略带诙谐的成分，但由此亦可见儒学对世界语言文化和哲学的影响非同一般。然而，从翻译的角度来看，读者都知道"孔子曰"与"孔子说"(Confucius says)的表达法在文体上和语义上可以说是"不可同日而语"，其中文化内涵的差异这里且不赘述。

孔子思想在中国文化土壤中生成，其中很多概念有其文化和历史的独特性; 加上中西(英)语言的差异，都给都给翻译带来了一定的难度，对翻译的准确度带来了挑战。首先，孔子思想中的"仁"，译文本身是回译，所以就将原文的"good"自然而然地就译成了"仁"，况且有《论语》可以参阅。然而读者可以看到，这里"仁"有两个译法，"humaneness"和"good"。试想一下，如果不是有《论语》可做参考，有多少译者会将这两个词译为"仁"呢？又有多少译者会将柏拉图的"idea of the good"或"form of the good"译为"仁之理念"或"仁之形式"呢？即使译成"仁"，这也是有待商榷的。而这仅仅是事物的一面，这里我们要重点考虑的是如何将中国的哲学概念恰当地译成英文。将"仁"译为"good"很可能是受了西方哲学概念的影响或启发，然而孔子的"仁"与西方哲学中的"goodness"是有差异的，并不是对等的。西方哲学中"good"的概念是抽象并且是模糊的，而孔子的"仁"则是有其具体内容的，是一个相对明确的概念。

"仁"的语义定义在英文中的表达可谓广泛，其中主要的包括kindness, benevolence, goodness, compassion, social conscience, charity, charitableness, humanity, philanthropism, generosity, magnanimity, liberality, beneficence等等，都似乎沾边，也都不尽然，且没有哪一个可以传递"仁"的要素，例如, 孝(filial piety)、悌(respect for elder brothers)、忠(loyalty)、恕(sympathy)、礼(ritual/

etiquette)、知(knowledge)、勇(gallantry)、恭(humility)、宽(generosity)、信(honesty)、敏(diligence)、惠(charity)等。

在这种文化和哲学概念的翻译中，两种语言一对一的对等是极难达到的，尤其考虑到"仁"的概念在孔子思想中的核心地位。因此在翻译这类文章时，音译(transliteration)加脚注的方法可作为一个翻译策略来使用，可用拼音ren加上"仁"的定义和基本要素。我们看到原文中保留了"仁/Ren"这一词，这对专门从事中国研究的学者可能不是问题，可这对一些不懂中文的读者来说，还不够透明，不妨加一脚注使其更加清楚明了，这样也有助于在英语中建构ren的概念及定义，而最终成为英语的新词。当然在译文允许的情况下也可使用文中诠释的策略，这些策略同样适用于其它哲学概念的翻译。

另外，概念的翻译并不是一成不变的，例如，在鲁迅的作品中，"仁"被译为"benevolence"，这在众多词语中是一个大词，比起其它同义词来说它显得抽象，很符合故事的内涵，体现了文学的批评性。需要脚注的另一个原因就是有些概念是流动的，还以"仁"为例，春秋战国时期到现代社会"仁"的概念也是在不断的演变中，这里就不一一累述。

二、术语的翻译(translation of terminologies)

在翻译哲学文本时，术语的翻译尤为重要，特别是英译汉，英语中很多术语都是使用普通单词或由普通单词构成的，而中文中术语化的倾向很强。让我们看看译文中的一个例子：

ST:　Claiming himself as a constructive and systematic philosopher rather than a Sinologist (xii), Neville engages in this language problem in his insightful philosophical construction.

TT:　纳维尔认为自己不是一个汉学家，而是一个建构和系统哲学家(xii)，他在其富有洞见的哲学建构中对该语言问题亦进行了讨论。

每个学科领域的术语使用都不尽相同，哲学和宗教亦不例外。我们知道,"constructive"和"systematic"在通常的情况下可译为"建设性"和"系统性"，但在哲学领域里，这是哲学的两个分支或方法,所以译为"建构哲学"和"系统哲学"(有时亦被译为"体系哲学")比较准确,也能体现其术语性。另外我们在看一下两个似乎相近而又不尽然的例子：

ST:　Last, it is important to have a constructive philosophy of life.

让我们看看两个不同的译法：

TT1:　最后，重要的是要有一个建设性的人生哲学。

TT2:　最后，拥有一个积极的人生观是很重要的。

第一个翻译显然是过于刻板，但意思的传递还是基本到位的，第二个翻译就对原文吃得较透彻,译文较易理解,认识到"constructive philosophy"是一个日常用语,并非术语。这里我们要说的是，翻译同一个词对语境的考虑是翻译的重要一环，而原文的用意也应适当纳入考虑的范围，这在翻译哲学文本时尤为重要。在翻译中简单地语言代码进行转换,会造成译文晦涩难懂、文不达意, 致以造成理解错误, 带来无法估量的后果, 希望以后有机会能继续深入探讨这一问题。

另一个例子是对"Sinology"及"Sinologist"的翻译, 虽然可以译为"中国学"或"中国学学者", 但考虑这一词汇的特殊性, 我们还是将其译为"汉学"或"汉学家"为妥, 因为这一词多指中国语言文学或中国古代历史和文化的研究和这领域的学者, 这有便于区别研究现当代中国问题的学科, 也就是"中国学"(Chinese studies or China studies)。尤其考虑到后来出现的有别于"Sinology"的"New Sinology", 将"Sinology"译为"汉学"也赋予"New Sinology"(译为"后汉学", 或"新汉学")的中文译文以连贯性和互文性。

三、自译的问题

在此我们可以告诉读者, 这两篇书评是作者自译而成。自译是当前翻译学术界一个方兴未艾的研究领域, 自译在翻译当中是一个特殊领域, 无论在翻译实践还是翻译理论中一直备受争议。我们知道自译和他译的不同之处是在于创作主体以及翻译主体为同一体, 作者在对自己著作进行翻译时所用策略与他译有所不同, 可以说使用的翻译策略更为多样化和有机化, 从而增强了译文的延展性。所以自译对翻译理论及模式的研究以及微观翻译策略的应用都带来了挑战。在自译中, 译者可以通过比较, 在语言内部进行较大程度的探索和对比, 在双语境中寻找更佳的表达形式, 建立一种自我对话的模式, 从而达到信息量的最大化, 最终将译文的内在涵义延伸并发展。当然自译也并非是绝对理想的方式, 这可能要因人因文而异。我们希望读者能在以下几个例子中体会以上的论述。

例一

ST: Contemporary philosophers and China studies scholars exploring the possibilities of bridging Confucian wisdom and Western philosophy would be interested in joining the insightful conversation in Neville's latest book *Ritual and Deference: Extending Chinese Philosophy in a Comparative Context*. The book is a collection of the author's invited lectures and essays, aimed at scholars of comparative philosophy.

TT: 纳维尔的新书《礼仪与敬意: 在比较的语境中延伸中国哲学》将吸引探讨儒学智慧与西方哲学架起沟通对话之桥的当代哲学家和中国学学者。这本书是作者一系列的讲座与文章的合集, 呈现比较哲学研究的思考。

例二

This book is focused on cultural interactions in funerals "in-between" Confucian and Christian traditions during a transitional period for China from the early 17th century.

钟鸣旦教授在《礼仪的交织: 明末清初中欧文化交流中的丧葬礼》一书中呈现了自17世纪早期转型时期的中国经历的中西文化交流与碰撞, 这样的文化碰撞特别体现在早期传教士和信教人士的丧葬礼中。

例三

To continue the metaphor in this book, the author is weaving various texts from late Ming and Qing China into the narration of the gradual transformation of Chinese funeral practices in some communities that had accepted Christian teachings.

继续这个编织机的隐喻，本书将明末到清代中国的不同文本编织到当时接受了天主教教义的人群的葬礼的渐变叙述中。

从以上例子我们可以看到在翻译较为复杂的社科和哲学文本时自译的一些策略的特点，尤其在句子结构方面有其独特的性质，很值得我们进行深入地研究和探讨，这不但使翻译理论问题化，而且将给翻译研究和实践注入新的能量。在本译评结束前读者可能会问，题目中提到的翻译哲学在哪儿？当然翻译哲学是一个精深的课题，以上三点是否对翻译哲学的建构有所启示呢？我们是否能从中得到些启发呢？这还待有我们继续探讨。

DOI https://doi.org/10.24103/GCSS1.en.2015.9

Appendix B
Understanding China and engaging with Chinese people: Commemorating the 100th Anniversary of Professor Fei Xiaotong's Birth[1]

The London School of Economics and Political Science is holding an international conference to commemorate the birth of Professor Fei Xiaotong (Fei Hsiao-Tung 1910-2005), the famous sociologist, anthropologist, social activist and senior Chinese political leader, an Honorary Fellow and among the School's most distinguished alumni. The conference, entitled "Understanding China and Engaging with Chinese People", will take place at LSE on the 5th December 2010. It will be followed by a series of related seminars from 6th to 8th December given by some participants.

The Conference will examine the importance and relevance of Fei Xiaotong's academic contributions and policy studies, and focus on China both as a part of global society and as a culture undergoing dramatic change. It will explore relationships and interactions between Han and ethnic minorities and between Chinese and non-Chinese people, in a search for dynamic, integrated, multi-faceted insights. Comparative and historical perspectives are both represented. The aim of the Conference is to advance mutual understanding between human beings as a process of the "cultural awareness" promoted by Professor Fei Xiaotong in his later years.

The Conference is a public event, open to academics, politicians, policy makers, consultants, professionals and practitioners of different kinds of businesses. It is jointly organized by Asia Research Centre, Department of Anthropology, China in Comparative Perspective Network (CCPN), Confucius Institute for Business London (CIBL) at LSE, together with Zhejiang UK Association (ZJUKA), and the School of Sociology and Anthropology, Sun Yat-sen University, China. It is supported by the Chinese Embassy in the UK, and sponsored by Hanban, Tsin-

---

[1] Editor's note: This is the collected information about a four-day event commemorating the 100th Anniversary of Professor Fei Xiaotong's Birth. It consisted of a one-day conference followed by three seminars. All information stated here was correct at time of posting to the CCPN LSE website in 2010.

ghua University, and Sun Yat-sen University. The Sino-UK Educational Service Centre will take responsibility for logistics.

International conference

Time and date: 9:00am-18:00pm, 5th December 2010, Sunday

Venue: New Theatre, EAS171, East Building, LSE

Chairs: Professor Stephan Feuchtwang and Dr Kent Deng, LSE

Organisers:

Asia Research Centre, LSE
Department of Anthropology, LSE
China in Comparative Perspective Network (CCPN),
Confucius Institute for Business London (CIBL), LSE
Zhejiang UK Association (ZJUKA), UK
School of Sociology and Anthropology, Sun Yat-sen University, China

Convenors: Dr Xiangqun Chang, LSE; Professor Daming Zhou, Sun Yat-sen University, China

Contact details: +44(0)2080994815; +44 (0) 20 7955 7603; ccpn@lse.ac.uk

Conference programme

9:00-13:00	Morning session - Chair: Professor Stephan Feuchtwang, Department of Anthropology; Director of China in Comparative Perspective Programme, LSE
9:00-9:30	Registration
9:30-9:35	Welcome, Professor Danny Quah, Department of Economics; Co-Director of the LSE Global Governance, LSE [PPT in English; Chinese coming soon...]
9:35-10:10	Guest speeches
	Mr WU Xun: Minister Counsellor, Chinese Embassy to the UK [Speech notes in Chinese; English coming soon...]
	Sir Howard Davies: LSE Director [Video speech in English]
	Professor George Gaskell: LSE Pro-Director
	Professor Hengsheng Zheng: Honorary President of the Chinese Sociological Association; Former vice President of Renmin University of China [Speech notes in Chinese; and English]
	Dr Ruth Kattumuri, Co-Director of the Asia Research Centre, LSE, UK [PPT]

Professor Lizhong Xie: Head of Department of Sociology and Institute of Sociology & Anthropology, Peking University, China [Speech Note in Chinese and English]

Professor Yongping Zhou, China Youth University for Political Sciences (CYUPS), on behalf of Ms Zonghui Fei: Fei's Xiaotong's only daughter [Speech notes in Chinese and English]

10:10-10:15   Group photo (all welcome)

10:15-10:30   Tea/Coffee break

10:30-11:00   What Western social scientists can learn from the writings of Fei Xiaotong? by Professor Gary G. Hamilton, University of Washington, Seattle, USA [PPT]

11:00-11:30   Moulüe – Supraplanning: On the problem of the transfer of earthbound words and concepts in the cultural exchange between China and the West, by Professor Harro von Senger, University of Freiburg; Swiss Institute of Comparative Law, Lausanne, Switzerland [Paper]

11:30-11:50   Fei Xiaotong and the continuation of the tradition of "'Chinese learning as the foundation, Western learning for utility", by Dr Kent Deng, LSE, UK [PPT]

11:50-12:20   Guanxi, Strategy and Cultural Awareness, by Professor Chien CHIAO, Shih Hsin University, Taiwan [Speech notes in English; paper in Chinese]

12:20-12:30   Discussant: Professor Christopher Howe, University of Sheffield; SOAS

12:30-13:00   Q&A

13:00-14:00   Lunch

14:00-18:00   Afternoon session - Chair: Dr Kent Deng, Department of Economic History, Co-Director of China in Comparative Perspective Network, LSE

14:00-14:20   Contributions to anthropological village studies through a comparison of two classic Chinese village studies by Daniel Kulp and Fei Xiaotong respectively, by Professor Daming Zhou, Sun Yat-sen University, China [PPT]

14:20-14:40   Similarities and differences: a comparison between "family properties" in rural Japan and China based on fieldwork in Kaixiangong Village, by Dr Hong Park, Hokkaido University, Japan [PPT]

14:40-15:10   From Fei Xiaotong's chaxugeju to lishang-wanglai – a social-cultural perspective on "China model", by Dr Xiangqun Chang, China in Comparative Perspective Network (CCPN), LSE, UK [PPT]

15:10-15:20   Discussant: Professor Maurice Bloch, Department of Anthropology, LSE

15:20-15:45   Q&A

15:45-16:00   Tea/Coffee break

16:00-16:20   The Interpretation of Fei Xiaotong and Ebenezer Howard's Thoughts on Migration Flows and Urbanization, by Mr Cary Z Woo, Renmin University of China; Chicago University, USA: Presented by Dr Ye Liu, Faculty of Policy and Society, Institute of Education, UoL, UK [PPT]

16:20-16:40   Rethinking of Multiple Maternities in Ethnic Minorities' Areas of China: A new perspective and thought from Fei Xiaotong's research on Ethnic Minorities in China, by Professor Wenjiong Yang, Lanzhou University, China; and LSE, UK [PPT]

16:40-17:10   Fei Xiaotong's life tribulations and contributions to academe and society, by Professor R. David Arkush, Department of History, University of Iowa, USA [Paper]

17:10-17:20   Discussant: Professor HW de Burgh, Director, China Media Centre, University of Westminster

17:20-17:45   Q&A

17:45-18:00   Closing remarks, by Professor Stephan Feuchtwang

A series of seminars

Date: 6th Dec Mon

Time: 19:00-21:00

Venue: NAB.2.04, LSE

Speakers: Professor Yongping Zhou, Head of Institute for Youth Development of China, China Youth University for Political Sciences (CYUPS), China; Ms Chenshu Zhou, Stanford University, USA

Chair: Dr Kent Deng, Reader in Economic History, Co-Director of China in Comparative Perspective Network, LSE

Title: Income and stratification: Kaixiangong Village from 1936 to 2010 [PPT in English and Chinese]

Date: 7th Dec Tue

Time: 19:00-21:00

Venue: NAB.1.15 , LSE

Speakers: LIU Xiuqin, Associate Professor, College of Economics & Management, South China Agricultural University (SCAU); MA Di, School of Finance, Central University of Finance and Economics (CUFE), China

Chair: Dr Xiangqun Chang, Research Fellow, Coordinator of China in Comparative Perspective Network, LSE

Title: Changes of organizational social capital during growth of agricultural enterprises: A case study [PPT in Chinese]

Date: 8th Dec Wed

Time: 19:00-21:00

Venue: NAB.1.07, LSE

Speaker: Professor Changli Bu, Department of sociology, Changchun University of Science and Technology, China

Chair: Dr Xiangqun Chang, Research Fellow, Coordinator of China in Comparative Perspective Network, LSE

Title: The new features of community conflict in Chinese cities [PPT in English]

Biographies of conference speakers

Professor R. David Arkush (欧达伟): Professor of History, University of Iowa, author of *Land Without Ghosts: Chinese Impressions of America from the Mid-Nineteenth Century to the Present* (University of California Press, co-ed. & trans. 1989; paperback ed. 1993); *Fei Xiaotong and Sociology in Modern China*, Harvard East Asian Monograph Series, 1981; Chinese ed. Beijing: Current Affairs Press, 1986)

Professor Changli Bu: Department of sociology, Changchun University of Science and Technology

Dr Xiangqun Chang (常向群): Research Fellow and Coordinator of China in Comparative Perspective Network (CCPN). Author of *Guanxi or Li shang wanglai? Reciprocity, Social Support Networks, & Social Creativity in a Chinese Village*, and its Chinese version in traditional characters, Airiti Press Inc. 2010; Chinese version in simplified characters, Liaoning People's publishing House; *Study of Fei Xiaotong's theories and restudies on Kaixiangong Village*, Foreign Language and Teaching Research Press, 2011.

Professor Chien CHIAO (乔健): Chair Professor of Anthropology, Shih Hsin University, Taiwan. Ph.D. in Anthropology from Cornell University (1969). Formally taught at Indiana University (1966-76), The Chinese University of Hong Kong (1976-95) where he founded the only Department of Anthropology in Hong Kong, and National Dong Hwa University (1995-2005) where he founded the Institute of Ethnic Relations and Culture and helped to build the College for Indigenous Studies. He was also the founder of Hong Kong Anthropological Society (1978) and International Association of Yao Studies (1988). He has authored and edited more than 34 books and published more than 60 articles.

Dr Kent G Deng (邓钢): Reader in Economic History, Co-Director of China in Comparative Perspective Network (CCPN). Author of Deng, Kent (1999) *The premodern Chinese economy: structural equilibrium and capitalist sterility*, Routledge, New York, 1999; co-editor of Technology in China, Continuum, 2009.

Professor Gary G. Hamilton (韩格理): Professor of Sociology and The Jackson School of International Studies University of Washington; Emergent Economies, Divergent Paths: Economic Organization and International Trade in South Korea and Taiwan, Cambridge University Press, 2006; translator of Fei Xiaotong's book *Xiangtu Zhongguo* (*From the Soil: the Foundations of Chinese Society*, University of California Press, 1992)

Dr Hong Park (朴红): Associate Professor, Agricultural Economics Division of Bio Resource and Product Science, Graduate School of Agriculture, Hokkaido University, Japan. She has published a numbers of books in Japanese, e.g. *The Revival of Family Business and Establishment of Rural Organizations in Northeast Rural China* (1999); *Peasant Association in China* (2001); *The Export Strategy of Vegetable Processing Enterprises in China* (2006); *Rural Cooperatives in Taiwan* (2010).

Professor Harro von Senger (胜雅律): Professor of Sinology, University of Freiburg, and the Swiss Institute of Comparative Law at Lausanne, author of *The Book of Stratagems: Tactics for Triumph and Survival*, Penguin, 1993; *The 36 Stratagems for Business: Achieve Your Objectives Through Hidden and Unconventional Strategies and Tactics*, Cyan Books, 2006.

Mr Cary Zhiming Woo (吴志明): Research Student in Renmin University of China, Visiting Scholar in University of Chicago; Coordinator of Fiscal Austerity and Urban Innovation Project in China. Published more than 10 journal articles, e.g. "The Interpretation of Fei Xiaotong and Ebenezer Howard's Thoughts on Migration Flows and Urbanization," *Urban Studies* (in Chinese), 2010 and etc.

Professor Wenjiong Yang (杨文炯): Professor of Centre for Studies of Ethnic Minorities, School of History and Culture, Lanzhou University; Visiting Senior Fellow of Department of Anthropology, LSE. Author of *Interaction, Adaptation and Reconstruction – Muslim Communities and Cultural Changes in Northwest Cities in China* (in Chinese), Nationalities Publishing House, 2007; 'The Historical base of Fei Xiaotong's "Pattern of Pluralistic Unity" – Historical and Anthropological perspectives', *Journal of Guansu United Universities*, 2006(6).

Professor Daming Zhou (周大鸣): Professor of Anthropology, Deputy Head of the School of Sociology and Anthropology; Director of Ethnic Group Study Centre; Sun Yat-Sen University; Editor of *Chinese Sociology Anthropology* (in English). Author of *Changes of Phoenix Village – Restudy Daniel Kulp's Phoenix Village* (in Chinese), Beijing: Social Science Press, 2006; *Say Goodbye to Rural Society – Rural Development 30 Years in Guangdong Province* (in Chinese), Guangdong People's Publishing House, 2008.

Other particulars

Weblisting about the event:

The London School of Economics and political Science:
http://www2.lse.ac.uk/publicEvents/events/2010/20101205t0900vLSE.aspx

Asia Research Centre, LSE:
http://www2.lse.ac.uk/asiaResearchCentre/events/individual/2010/101205-Conference.aspx

Department of Anthropology, LSE:
http://www2.lse.ac.uk/anthropology/events/Conferences/understanding-China-2010.aspx

China in Comparative Perspective Network (CCPN), LSE:
English version:
http://www2.lse.ac.uk/anthropology/research/CCPN/newsEvents/CCPN/2010/Fei_Xiaotong/FeiConference_en.aspx

Chinese Version:
http://www2.lse.ac.uk/anthropology/research/CCPN/ChineseSite/newsEvents/Fei/FeiConference_cn.aspx

Confucius Institute for Business London (CIBL), LSE:
http://www.lse.ac.uk/collections/confuciusInstitute/events/Default.htm

Zhejiang UK Association (ZJUKA): http://www.zjuka.org.uk/page12.html

School of Sociology and Anthropology, Sun Yat-sen University, China:
http://www.anthrop.org.cn/school/Item/2820.aspx .

Outcome:

The conference working language is English. Please submit the title and abstract of your talk by the 15th November; speech notes (2000-3000 words) and full paper up to 6000 words including notes and references by 31 November.

All the speeches, discussant notes and presentations will be published as conference proceedings in English, Chinese both simplified and traditional characters. Editors are Stephan Feuchtwang, Xiangqun Chang, Kent Deng and Daming Zhou.

Fees:

The conference is free, but the cost for participating in the event will be responsible by yourself except invited guests and speakers. We will send you official invitation letter and detailed arrangements once we received your registration form.

CCPN will pass all the logistic details to the Sino-UK Educational Service.

The registration is still need it for those who don't request travel and accommodations, because we need the details to book tea/coffee and lunch for all the participants during the conference, and network with them after the conference.

Registration: To complete the online registration form you can receive an immediately confirmation for acceptance to attend the conference before 30 November.

Registration form (omitted)

DOI https://doi.org/10.24103/GCSS1.en.2015.10.1

Appendix C
Guest Speeches at the Event in Honour of the Centenary of Fei Xiaotong's Birth at LSE

LSE MSc China in comparative perspective is a kind of tribute to Fei Xiaotong

Sir Howard Davies' speech[1]

I'm glad to know that the school is organizing this conference in honour of Fei Xiaotong. He is of course our most eminent and certainly longest lasting Chinese alumnus. He came to the school in 1936 and worked with Bronislaw Malinowski for a couple of years here. And we like to think that his time at the LSE was influential in all his subsequent work on anthropology and understanding Chinese society. Of course, now, we have a very large number of Chinese students in the school – over 600 at any one time. But in the 1930s, he was undoubtedly a rare presence in the school. We had very few people then from mainland China. Now I know that many of our alumni look up to him as someone who worked hard to understand China in the light of what he learned in the West. We now have a course in school called China in Comparative Perspective, which in a way can be seen as a kind of tribute to his work, trying to understand China but using the perspectives from other parts of the world. And I think that very much is in the tradition of his work. So it's excellent that on the centenary of his birth we are able to bring together such a lot of people to talk about his academic heritage. I think it's very important for the LSE to keep in touch with the influence of the people who passed through here. I hope you all have an interesting and a rewarding day.

---

[1] Sir Howard Davies was the Director of the London School of Economics and Political Science from 2003 to 2011. He is now Chairman of Royal Bank of Scotland (RBS). Sir Howard Davies was in Paris during the conference period. Professor George Gaskell, the then LSE pro-director, represented the school and made a welcome speech. A video of Sir Howard's speech was played at the conference. This is a transcription of the speech.

DOI https://doi.org/10.24103/GCSS1.en.2015.10.2

Fei Xiaotong's desire of enriching people and global economics[2]

Danny Quah[3]

1. Introduction

Distinguished guests:

Welcome to this international conference at LSE on 'Understanding China and Engaging with Chinese People', on the occasion of the 100th anniversary of the birth of Professor Fei Xiaotong. It is my great pleasure and honour to get to deliver these opening remarks to this remarkable gathering of scholars, put together by my friends and colleagues here at LSE and elsewhere.

From here at LSE in London, I have recently been able to develop ever stronger personal and institutional ties with both Beida and Qinghua in Beijing. But I never had the honour of meeting Professor Fei, despite his own close connections with these same three institutions of higher learning. I know of course of Professor Fei's work in sociology and anthropology, both developing these fields within China itself and, conversely, introducing Chinese experiences in these areas to scholars internationally.

Today's conference on 'Understanding China and Engaging with Chinese People' rightly emphasizes the sociology and anthropology that so occupied Professor Fei throughout his academic career. It is there that Professor Fei's intellectual contributions continue to find resonance. At this current international, political and business juncture, it is appropriate also for me to say a few words about economics, relating to Fei's lifelong pursuit of enriching people, to 'understand China and engage with its people'.

2. China's Place in the Global Economy

To begin, take the big picture in global economic performance or the basic welfare proposition for humanity: out there in the world, poverty and hunger go hand in hand. China in the quarter century after 1980 successfully lifted 627 million people out of grinding poverty, more than the entire world was able to do in that same time. That the global economy sees poverty reduction well on its way to meeting the first of the UN's Millennium Development Goals – to halve, between

---

[2] This is an opening remark of the conference. The title is added by the editors.
[3] Danny Quah is Professor of Economics and International Development at LSE and Director of the Saw Swee Hock Southeast Asia Centre at LSE's Institute of Global Affairs.

1990 and 2015, the rate of extreme poverty in the world – is due to the economic performance of a single country, China.

True, China remains today a still-poor emerging economy. At market exchange rates, China's per capita income remains just one-fifteenth that of the US. But over the last two world economic downturns before the 2008 global financial crisis, even as the US economy slowed sharply in 1991 and 2001, it was China that continued to drive global economic growth – contributing to growth in the world economy in absolute terms three times and one and a half times, respectively, the absolute growth in US output (again at market exchange rates). It has been China, therefore, that has crucially stabilized the global economy in past episodes of economic downturn.

For now, not all the numbers are yet in on recovery from the 2008 global financial crisis. But it is an almost-sure proposition that again China and, in perspective, the rest of East Asia will be seen to continue to power growth in the global economy overall.

It is the absolute size of this momentum in the East that has driven the world's economic centre of gravity from mid-Atlantic in 1980 eastwards past Izmir in Turkey by 2010, three-quarters of the Earth's radius in three decades. One extrapolation has it that by 2050 that centre of gravity will have continued to move east to locate between India and China, a total shift of 9,800 km or one and a half times the planet's radius, from 1980.

Of course, in December 2010, the global economy sees risk not just from financial crisis and economic downturn, significant though these undoubtedly are. Today, the hazards from global climate change loom ever more sharply. But arguably here too, despite its still being a developing country, China has already assumed global leadership. In the area of renewable energy, by 2008 China had already become the world's largest manufacturer of solar panels; by 2009, of wind turbines. By early 2011, China will likely be producing two thirds of the world's solar panels.

Already, Xi'an, the capital of Shanxi province, is the location for the latest, largest research laboratory for the world's biggest supplier of equipment and materials for semiconductors, solar panels and flat panel displays. Xi'an too is the location for world-leading research in cleaner coal technology. Tianjin, in northeast China, hosts the world's largest wind turbine manufacturing complex and large-scale experimental eco-city living.

If all these – solar panels, wind turbines and clean coal technologies – are produced in China so efficiently and so cheaply that the resulting energy flow becomes priced competitively compared to regular fossil fuel, cries of unfair competition from less efficient producers elsewhere will sound ever more shrill and unconvincing. There is after all a world to save.

3. Conclusion

The lesson I draw from this is that the divide between West and East is, in the final global analysis, irrelevant. We should be concerned only with what works efficiently. But that's an idealistic economist speaking. In the real world, domestic concerns trump global imperatives. So, we will continue to need sharp analysis and policy guidance – learning from East to West and West to East – as the global economy seeks to navigate global climate change, currency wars, a shaky international financial architecture and continued misapprehension with global economic and soft power both continuing to shift.

'Understanding China and engaging with Chinese people' have never been more important.

DOI https://doi.org/10.24103/GCSS1.en.2015.10.3

In social science: one plus one doesn't equal two

WU Xun[4]

Good morning, ladies and gentlemen:

It is my honour to participate in today's academic conference, hosted by the London School of Economics and Political Science in memory of Fei Xiaotong's centenary.

Fei Xiaotong is a well-known sociologist, anthropologist and social activist in China. Most of his work has had a lasting influence on the development of China's socio-anthropology. His contribution to social reform, social development and the policy of opening up China is marvellous.

The United Kingdom has played an important role in Fei's life. He studied in the UK when he was young. His dissertation for his degree at the London School of Economics was entitled Peasant Life in China, which is considered a fine example of the development of China's socio-anthropology.

Fei Xiaotong appreciates the spirit of valuing practice that focuses on reality and real actions, which can be found in the English people. Also, he thinks highly of undertaking work in the field and integrating theory with practice in doing sociological research.

Social science is different from practical science. In social science, one plus one does not have to equal two. It may be more or less than two. This idea also applies to how we get along with one another as individuals, nations and ethnicities. And research on socio-anthropology has played a crucial role in communication between and understanding one another. 'Understanding China and Engaging with the Chinese People' is the topic of today's conference.

Today, marking the centenary of Fei Xiaotong's birth, this conference brings significance to the further discussion of Fei's theories and will help different countries and nations to better understand one another.

---

[4] WU Xun, Minister Counsellor, Cultural Section, Chinese Embassy to the UK (2007-13); he was Director of American and Outreach Office at the Ministry of Culture (2004-06).

DOI https://doi.org/10.24103/GCSS1.en.2015.10.4

One Monument, One Road, and One Era

ZHENG Hangsheng[5]

Good Morning (Afternoon), Ladies and gentlemen:

Today, here at the grand commemoration of Mr Fei Xiaotong's centenary, I should like, on behalf of the Chinese Sociological Association, to express three ideas, namely that Mr Fei Xiaotong represents one academic monument, one academic road and one academic era in Chinese sociology. He also represents an academic bridge for sociological communication and exchange between China and the West. Today's international conference is vivid proof of this fact.

One Academic Monument

Whether because of his academic contributions to sociology or his role in advancing sociology, we can say that Mr Fei represents one academic monument in Chinese sociology.

With respect to his academic contributions to sociology, Mr Fei earnestly practised the sinolization of sociology, diligently pursuing the rights and power of academic discourse, creating a series of new terms, such as 'earthbound society,' 'ripple-style structure', 'plural-ethnicity in one-state of the Chinese nation', 'small-town big-issue' and 'cultural self-consciousness', which have now become part of the collective memory in Chinese sociology circles, as well as precious academic resources. In Peasant Life in China, Mr Fei made the differences between the civilized and the savage in social anthropology relative, transferring research objectives from the primitive or savage society to agricultural and civilized society. He also advocated that we should appreciate ourselves, appreciate others and appreciate one another. If we did so, the world would become harmonious. This thought expressed a new idea of civilization, which will have ever greater effects on international cultural communications and dialogue among civilizations in future. He put forward the theory of the expanding sociological boundary, according to which sociology includes both scientific and humanist characteristics. This theory has posed a great challenge to the scientificism of positivists in sociology, demonstrating the correct direction for the development of Chinese sociology.

With respect to advancing the discipline of sociology, especially in reviving and reconstructing Chinese sociology, he and Madam Lei Jieqiong played unparalleled roles. Although the trend towards reviving and reconstructing Chinese sociology was irresistible against the background of domestic and international

---

[5] Zheng Hangsheng (1936–2014) was the founder of Chinese sociology in the modern period. He was an Honorary President of the Chinese Sociological Association and Vice-president of Renmin University of China.

development, we sociologists still feel grateful to Deng Xiaoping, who took a decisive political role in grasping the trend, and to Mr Fei and Madam Lei, who promoted it.

One Academic Road

A monument is a static concept. If, by contrast, we take a dynamic perspective, we can see that Mr Fei also represents one road, a road that Chinese sociologists should follow. The direction of this road is 'to base upon reality, to develop traditions, to learn and reference from foreign countries and to create Chinese characteristics'.

Mr Fei took the reality of Chinese society as his base, his starting point and his destination throughout his life. Mr Fei inherited and pursued the tradition of serving society through Chinese sociology, as a way to strengthen the state and to make people prosperous, not for the sake of pure sociology, of 'academics only for academics'. He said, 'People of our generation think day and night how to make China strong, wealthy and powerful.'[6]. He took 'aiming to make people wealthy' to mean 'returning hospitality'[7], that is, sociology should repay Chinese society. He especially paid attention to field work, making excursion after excursion. His book Seeking Knowledge from Facts represents his attitude to the science of drawing every conclusion from the facts.[8].

In an essay entitled 'To inherit an excellent cultural tradition and to pour the spirit of the era into it', he expressed the aims of developing traditions. He had done as he said, as his paper 'The structure of plural ethnicity in one state of the Chinese nation' clearly showed. Concept and theory, which still form the framework and structure in national affairs in China today, are the results of inheriting an excellent historical tradition and pouring the spirit of the new era into it. This structure has a close connection with social operational thought directed at removing disorder and striving for order in China. In China, only the structure or mechanism of plural-ethnicity in one state can achieve this desirable condition.

With respect to learning from foreign counties, Mr Fei's approach was comparison, using lively descriptions and images. For example, when discussing the 'ripple-style structure', he compared earthbound China to circles of ripples spreading out from the centre, while the organizational structures of Western society were like bundles of firewood.

From all these aspects – basing findings upon reality, developing traditions, learning and referencing from foreign countries, dealing with the relationship between sociology and the social reality of China – Mr Fei realized a theoretical innovation.

---

[6] Fei, Xiaotung. 2005. *On Culture and Cultural Self-consciousness*. Qunyan Press p. 160.
[7] Ibid, p.276.
[8] Ibid, p.276.

One Academic Era

Whether viewed from the point of view of his academic contributions or his teaching experiences, Mr Fei formed one academic era.

All of us in Chinese sociological circles should prize the academic heritage Mr Fei bequeathed us, which is composed of one academic monument, one academic road and one academic era. This is a very precious heritage. As Mr Fei experienced different historical periods of China, his academic bequest has different meanings and values, which we should analyze in detail.

As we all know, Chinese society has changed greatly. China today is not the earthbound China of the 1930s and 1940s described by Mr Fei. Mr Fei himself was aware of these changes. Thus, if we still use the earthbound concept to describe the present reality, obviously this will lead nowhere. What we should learn from him is not the detailed description of past social phenomena but his spirit, concept and methodology of observing the world.

It is extremely important to note that Mr Fei was a scholar who could advance with the times. He invented some new terminologies and theories based on the reality of contemporary China, while also rethinking the past. I am afraid that we do not yet have a good grasp of these terminologies and theory, especially of the theory of the expanding sociological boundary, which enabled sociology to encompass scientific and humanist characteristics, and of his new ideas on culture and civilization.

Mr Fei's articles in which he rethought his ideas with the benefit of hindsight were written after 1995, when he was 85 years old. I believe these are worthy of our special attention. They represent conclusions from the experiences a lifetime and from his long-acquired wisdom. Our young successors can gain important enlightenment from these articles.

All in all, to develop the monument, to continue on the road and to engage in new practice in order to broaden our understanding, inheriting and developing our precious heritage, constitute the best commemoration for Mr Fei and demonstrate our esteem for it. We, especially our young scholars and teachers, the hope and future of Chinese sociology, should stand on the shoulders of Mr Fei, an academic giant, and continue to strive and climb upwards. I think it is just for this purpose that we are gathered together here today to commemorate Mr Fei's centenary. Thank you, everyone!

DOI https://doi.org/10.24103/GCSS1.en.2015.10.5

India-China community relations

Ruth Kattumuri[9]

I would first like to congratulate the organizers for this interesting conference to commemorate the birth centenary of Professor Fei Xiaotong.

From my reading of Professor Fei, I feel a sense of pride in acknowledging his remarkable courage and motivation reflected in his achievements, particularly as one of our LSE's own.

I am originally from the 'other' country with over 1 billion people. I have been involved in discussions with key policymakers in the last decade to encourage cooperation between India and China.

Engagement between Indians and Chinese has been growing in recent years. Bilateral trade has grown 30-fold since 2000. The total trade volume reached over $51 billion in 2008. I became aware of the phrase 'India–China bhai-bhai [meaning brothers]' in the 1970s. A headline after a trade fair in 2010 read 'India–China buy-bye', indicating that not only were the levels of trade high but also the transactions were completed so quickly that the Chinese traders were able to leave before the trade fair officially ended. The India Pavilion (pictured) at Shanghai Expo 2010 was extremely popular.

The leaders of both countries are involved in greater political engagement. Prime Minister Manmohan Singh said on 27 October 2010, 'There is enough economic space in the world to accommodate the growth ambitions of both India and China.' On 29 October, Prime Minister Wen Jiabao echoed this sentiment, saying, 'There is enough space in the world for India and China to achieve common development and to have cooperation. We must strive to ensure the sound and steady growth of our relationship.' The year 2010 marked the 60th anniversary of India–China diplomatic relations. President Pratibha Patil visited China and dedicated an Indian-style Buddhist stupa as a gift to the people of China. This sits adjacent to the White Horse Temple in Luoyang.

Relationships are developed through state policies as well as through the economic exchanges and social interactions among people and communities. There is tangible evidence of growing economic and social relations in the last few years. Since the early 2000s, feng shui rakhis (bracelets) have been sold in India. Rakhi is an inherently Indian festival marking a tradition where a sister ties a rakhi on her brother's hand. Shopping in Chinese markets has become increasing popular. Chinese dolls are being sold in traditional Indian classical musical instruments stores, even in Chennai in south India. Indian–Chinese couples are getting mar-

---

[9] Dr Ruth Kattumuri is Co-Director of Asia Research Centre and the India Observatory London School of Economics and Political Science.

ried, which will further strengthen and develop the relationships between the two peoples.

I believe that Professor Fei, who focused on the functional interrelationships of various 'parts' of a community and on the meaning of a culture as seen by its members, promoted cooperation between our two ancient and rich cultures. And I hope that the cooperation between India and China will continue to be enhanced. I wish the conference, focusing on Professor Fei's great tradition and thoughts, every success.

DOI https://doi.org/10.24103/GCSS1.en.2015.10.6

Peking University – starting and ending points of Fei Xiaotong's academic career

Xie Lizhong[10]

Good morning!

Today, I am honoured to have the opportunity to join friends from around the world in London to commemorate the 100th anniversary of the birth of Fei Xiaotong. First of all, I would like to pay the highest respects to and cherish the memory of Professor Fei Xiaotong on behalf of the Department of Sociology, Peking University.

Eighty years ago, in order to seek the means of saving his motherland, Fei Xiaotong came to Yanching University from Soochow University to study sociology. In 1985, a long half-century later, he returned to his alma mater, which is now part of Peking University, also known as Yan Yuan. After returning to the beautiful Yan Yuan campus by the famous Weiming Lake, he devoted the last 20 years of his career to Peking University, giving lectures and directing postgraduate students. In an article commemorating the 90th anniversary of Peking University, Prof. Fei wrote: 'The melody of my life in the world of sociology began at Weiming Lake, and now I have returned to Weiming Lake to continue composing the rest of the melody. Peking University, which includes the old Yenching University that gave birth to my academic career, offered me teaching I will never forget. In my old age, I am so happy to return to her arms.' These words show the deep affection Prof. Fei had for Peking University. This is the honour and pride of Peking University.

Seventy-four years ago, in order to learn about the advanced theories and methods of Western social science and to promote the development of sociology and anthropology in China, Professor Fei Xiaotong came to the London School of Economics and studied under Professor Malinowski. Professor Malinowski taught him a set of functionalist theories and methods of anthropology, which was quite different from the structure-functionalism of sociology that was later popular in Europe and other countries. He brought the new theories and methods he learned in London back to China. Throughout his career, he further complemented and promoted the theory of functionalism in the context of China, and preserved and developed this unique academic tradition in Chinese sociology and anthropology research. This is the heritage that Professor Fei Xiaotong bequeathed to sociology and anthropology in China and the rest of the world. We should cherish it. Here,

---

[10] XIE Lizhong is Professor of Sociology and former Head of the Department of Sociology and Institute of Sociology and Anthropology, Peking University, China.

I wish to express our heartfelt thanks to the London School of Economics, the other alma mater of Professor Fei Xiaotong, on behalf of the sociologists and anthropologists of Peking University. Thank you for accepting and training such a brilliant student from China, thank you for your contribution to the development of modern social science in China by providing excellent education and training to Chinese social science researchers like Professor Fei, and facilitating the propagation of the ideas of modern social science into China. I sincerely hope the academic exchange and friendship between the scholars of Peking University and the London School of Economics that was pioneered by Professor Malinowski and Professor Fei, later advanced by Professor Feuchtwang and others, can be further solidified and developed.

Although Professor Fei has left us, his reputation and academic ideas have already spread around the world. As a great scholar, his academic contributions are of great value not only to China but also to the world. His book From the Soil enabled the world to better understand China's particular social structure; his Peasant Life in China defined the mode of production of China from a different perspective; the framework he proposed of 'the plurality and unity of the Chinese people' has become an important theoretical framework for understanding ethnic relations in Chinese history; his concept of 'cultural awareness' and his ideal of globalization – a harmonious world of 'Datong: all these are gaining more and more acceptance. As long as the concept of From the Soil is alive, the model of Peasant Life in China is alive, the framework of 'plurality and unity' is alive, the spirit of 'cultural awareness' is alive, and the pursuit of a 'harmonious world' is alive, then, I believe, Professor Fei is and will forever be alive in our hearts.

Thank you all!

DOI https://doi.org/10.24103/GCSS1.en.2015.10.7

An address from Fei Xiaotong's daughter[11]

Fei Zonghui

Ladies and gentlemen,

You travelled here from around the world to attend this conference today, which commemorates the 100th anniversary of my father's birth. On behalf of my husband and my children, I would like to extend our most sincere thanks to the organizers of the conference.

The world-renowned London School of Economics held an especially important place in my father's life. Following the guidance of his mentor, Bronislaw Malinowski, my father entered the world of anthropology through the door opened by the London School of Economics. Thus it is especially meaningful to commemorate his 100th anniversary here through this conference. However, it is a great pity that my husband and I are unable to attend, owing to health reasons.

Although I am not familiar with the specialized theories of anthropology and sociology, I understand my father's goals and ideals in his devotion to the two disciplines. He hoped that his academic work could help Chinese people become wealthier and promote communication and understanding among different cultures in the world. He hoped to create a better society.

I believe that this conference will carry on my father's wishes and make great contributions to the cultural exchange between the East and the West.

I would like to offer the newest edition of the Complete Works of Fei Xiaotong and a latest English/Chinese bilingual version of Peasant Life in China as gifts to my father's alma mater. It is my hope that, through the academic platform provided by the London School of Economics, my father's ideas will continue to be disseminated around the world.

I wish everyone good health, and wish the conference huge success.

---

[11] FEI Zonghui is Fei Xiaotong's only daughter. Fei Zonghui was too ill to visit the UK. On her behalf, Professor Yongping Zhou, Fei's first PhD student at Peking University, read the letter and presented her gifts – Fei Xiaotong completed work (20 volumes) to the LSE.

DOI https://doi.org/10.24103/GCSS1.en.2015.11

Appendix D

A report on the Event in Honour of the Centenary of Fei Xiaotong's Birth

Jing Xu[1]

To commemorate the centenary of Professor Fei Xiaotong's (Fei Hsiao-Tung 1910–2005) birth, the London School of Economics and Political Science (LSE) held an international conference on 5 December and a series of seminars from 6 to 8 December. Fei was a celebrated sociologist, anthropologist, social activist and senior Chinese political leader. At LSE he was an Honorary Fellow and one of the school's most distinguished alumni. The events were entitled 'Understanding China and Engaging with Chinese People', and were organized by the Asia Research Centre (LSE), the Department of Anthropology (LSE), China in Comparative Perspective Network (CCPN, LSE), Zhejiang UK Association (ZJUKA) and the School of Sociology and Anthropology, Sun Yat-sen University, China.

Despite the chilly weather, more than 200 people travelled from China, Taiwan, Japan, USA, Switzerland, Belgium, Netherlands, Spain and many cities in the UK to attend this conference. They included academics and students, politicians, policy makers, consultants, professionals and practitioners of various kinds of businesses. The conference was opened by a welcome speech from Professor Danny Quah (Co-director of LSE Global Governance Centre). Following him, Mr Xun Wu, Minister Counsellor of the Chinese Embassy to the UK, made a speech in which he recalled the first time his father, a professor at Wuhan University, told him about Fei Xiaotong. After Sir Howard Davies's speech on video, Professor George Gaskell, the LSE Pro-director, made a speech representing the School. Professor ZHENG Hangsheng, former Vice-president of Renmin University of China, Honorary President of the Chinese Sociological Association (CSA) representing the CSA, Dr Ruth Kattumuri (Co-director of the Asia Research Centre, LSE) and Professor Lizhong Xie (Head of the Department of Sociology and Institute of Sociology and Anthropology, Peking University, China), also gave speech-

---

[1] Jing Xu is a UK-based social science researcher, with expertise in policy evaluation. She was former the Research Assistant of the CCPN at LSE.

es. Professor Yongping Zhou of China Youth University for Political Sciences addressed the conference on behalf of Ms Zonghui Fei, who was Fei's only daughter, unfortunately unable to attend the conference for health reasons. Zhou presented Ms Fei's gifts to her father's alma mater: an English–Chinese bilingual volume of present life in China, which was based on Fei's PhD dissertation at LSE in 1938, together with Fei's 20 volumes of completed work.

The conference focused on China both as a part of a global society and as a culture undergoing dramatic change. It examined the importance and relevance of Fei Xiaotong's academic contributions and policy studies from interdisciplinary and comparative perspectives. Professor Gary G. Hamilton (University of Washington, Seattle, USA), the translator of Fei's Xiangtu Zhongguo (From the Soil: the foundations of Chinese society, 1992), talked about what Western social scientists can learn from the writings of Fei Xiaotong; Professor Harro von Senger (University of Freiburg, Switzerland), taking the term of 'moulüe' as an example, analysed the problem of the transfer of 'sinological earthbound' words and concepts in the cultural exchange between China and the West. The conference culminated with LSE economic historian Dr Kent Deng's comparison between Fei Xiaotong and Mao Zedong, which provoked lively discussion among the attendees. Subsequently, Professor Chien Chiao returned us to the charming realm of anthropology with his slow but kind voice articulating his study of guanxi and strategy. In his discussion, Professor Christopher Howe also recalled his study of Fei's work at SOAS and the influence of Fei's work in Hong Kong, where he worked.

The presentations and discussions in the afternoon put the focus on a comparative perspective. Professor Daming Zhou from Sun Yat-sen University, China, talked about the 'contributions to anthropological village studies through a comparison of two classic Chinese village studies by Daniel Kulp and Fei Xiaotong, respectively'; Dr Hong Park from Hokkaido University, Japan, compared 'family properties' between rural Japan and China, based on fieldwork in Kaixiangong Village. Dr Xiangqun Chang, the CCPN coordinator, gave a presentation on the comparison between Fei Xiaotong's chaxugeju and her own work on lishang-wanglai, a socio-cultural perspective on the 'China model', which was very well received. On behalf of Mr Cary Z. Woo, Renmin University of China (who is visiting the USA), Dr Ye Liu, a CCPN research assistant, made a presentation comparing the work of Fei Xiaotong and Ebenezer Howard on migration flows and urbanization. Professor Wenjiong Yang, visiting fellow of Anthropology, LSE and Lanzhou University, China, presented a paper entitled 'Rethinking of multiple maternities in ethnic minority areas of China: a new perspective' and some thoughts from Fei Xiaotong's research on ethnic minorities in China. Finally, Professor R. David Arkush, author of Fei Xiaotong and Sociology in Revolutionary China (1981), reviewed Fei's work and life journey. In his discussion, Professor H. W. de Burgh, Director, China Media Centre, University of Westminster, succeeded superbly in drawing together common themes in these very different talks. The conference ended on an upbeat note with CCPN Director and chair of the conference, Professor Stephan Feuchtwang's closing remarks.

Following the international conference, three related seminars also took place at LSE from 6 to 8 December. On 6 December, Professor Yongping Zhou (Head of the Institute for Youth Development of China, China Youth University for Political Sciences, China) and Ms Chenshu Zhou (Stanford University, USA) ran a seminar on income and stratification in Kaixiangong Village from 1936 to 2010. Zhou was Professor Fei Xiaotong's first PhD student at Peking University. He is the author of Seventy Years in Kaixiangong Village. Based on this study, he stressed his enthusiasm for 'building a rational society and harmonious community' – a social development concept of China.

The second seminar, on 7 December, moved the focus from village study to the development of agricultural enterprises. The speakers were Associate Professor Liu Xiuqin from the College of Economics and Management, South China Agricultural University (SCAU), and Ms Ma Di from School of Finance, Central University of Finance and Economics, China. Because of heavy traffic congestion, the start of the seminar was delayed. However, in spite of a reduced number of participants, the seminar and discussion went well. The speakers argued that the development of agribusiness is a process of capital integration in which capital inherited from the family combines with rural social capital, which, meanwhile, has been continuously syncretizing capital from other social levels. The content and nature of the organization changes with different stages of the development of the enterprise. A high level of rural social capital plays a critical role in the emergence and development of native agribusiness by enabling organizations to conquer the double obstacles of limitations of capital and institutions that are at an early stage. Agribusiness achieves the necessary organizational efficiency by substituting the factor of hierarchy with the rural social capital integrant, including trust, regulation and networking. This talk tried to explain the existence and growth of non-typical hierarchical organizations and provide new insights into the status and the development of agribusiness.

The final seminar, on 8 December, moved the focus from rural to urban study. This discussion was based on 24 fieldwork cases of urban communities in the northeast of China. The study identified five new features of community conflict in present Chinese cities, that is, traits, types, extent, cause and solution. This attracted the interest of many scholars, notably Professor Stephan Feuchtwang, Anthropology, and Professor Jude Howell, Social Policy and Development Studies, LSE, and Professor Harriet Evans, from the University of Westminster, among others. In her talk, Professor Changli Bu (Professor of Sociology, Changchun University of Science and Technology, China) analysed the new features of community conflict in present Chinese cities, such as the trend towards diversity and complexity, which is different from that of the unit communities under the planning system. At the end of this talk, Professor Bu made a methodological comparison between Fei's community study and her new approach. After the presentation, many questions were raised from the audience; in particular, a qualified lawyer brought up several concrete questions on the role that lawyers play in mediating community conflicts and the direction of evolution of Chinese judicial institutions.

According to Dr Xiangqun Chang, the event convenor, this event demonstrated two characteristics. First, multi-disciplinary participation: speakers came from sociology, anthropology, ethnology, sinology, history, economic history, agricultural economics and management science and other disciplines. Second, the exercise of comparative perspective in various forms: Chinese and non-Chinese writings and thinking, the Chinese concept of moulüe and relevant terms in the West; the influence in Chinese society of Fei Xiaotong and Mao Zedong; Fei's concept of chaxugeju and its updated version lishang-wanglai; family property in rural Chinese and Japanese societies; Fei Xiaotong and Ebenezer Howard on migration flows and urbanization; income and social stratification in the 1930s when Fei did his fieldwork and in different historical periods; and community studies in rural and urban areas. This commemoration of Fei Xiaotong shows how Chinese scholars' social scientific studies on China can be introduced into general social scientific disciplines. The significance of the event in commemorating Fei Xiaotong was reflected by three aspects: (1) it called for the international academic community to re-examine Fei Xiaotong's academic contributions to human knowledge from the perspectives of fieldwork, methodology and theory; (2) it brought together scholars from China and other countries to discuss Fei Xiaotong's academic thoughts relating to their own work and thereby to deepen understanding of Chinese society; (3) it made a positive attempt in this direction by introducing Chinese social scientific products, which had relatively low recognition among international academics, to human knowledge.

Professor Fei chose to accept a historical responsibility for the Chinese nation and his fellow people. He spent almost his whole life advancing mutual understanding between human beings as a process of 'cultural awareness'. This was his life's pursuit. His own career ambition and academic specialty became as one with the country's prosperity, social progress and people's happiness. His work was always imbued with his modesty and objectivity, although he was neither humble nor proud and always gave priority to the facts, which well represents the noble spirit of an intellectual. His contributions to academic research and his humanity together constitute a valued treasure for us all.

DOI https://doi.org/10.24103/GCSS1.en.2015.12

Appendix E

Some Western Scholars Meeting Fei Xiaotong in the 1980's

Note by Bettina Gransow[1]**:** In 1981, the Freie Universität (FU) Berlin and Beijing University started an exchange programme and it happened that I was the first PhD student from FU to visit Beida, where I worked on my thesis on social classes and strata in the People's Republic of China (Gransow 1983). In spring 1981 I got the chance to meet Prof. Fei Xiaotong at Nankai University in Tianjin. He was accompanied by another faculty member. The conversation was in English, but when I asked something like, 'Would you describe contemporary Chinese society in terms of classes or in terms of social strata?', he murmured to his colleague: 龙生龙、凤生凤、老鼠生子 会打洞 ". I forgot his 'official' English answer, but always remember his whispered aside. He tried to convince me that my research topic was far too broad and that I had better choose some community or danwei (such as Peking University) as my research focus. He said, 'You, little girl, want to know about the whole world, but I am only an old man who researched a small village.' Years later, during the 1990s, I decided to compare migrant communities (urban villages) in Chinese metropolises. Maybe this was a late outcome of Prof. Fei's suggestion. Undoubtedly this first conversation with Fei Xiaotong reinforced my already great interest in the history of Chinese sociology, which then became the topic of my postdoctoral thesis (Gransow 1992). The history of Chinese sociology and particularly the preparation of my (short) visits to Kaixiangong and Kuige (in 1986) were the focus of my second visit (in 1985 or early 1986), this time to Fei's home in Beijing, together with my German colleague, Mechthild Leutner (see picture).

---

[1] Bettina Gransow is Professor of Chinese Politics at the East Asian Institute and the Otto-Suhr-Institut of Political Science, Free University of Berlin, Germany.

Bettina Gransow (right) and Mechthild Leutner with Fei Xiaotong, 1981

Note by Enzo Mingione[2]**:** Together with my colleague, Alberto Martinelli, I spent a memorable afternoon speaking with Fei at his invitation in 1984 at the National Assembly in Beijing. Although a long time has passed since that meeting, I have since read his works with great interest and pleasure.

Enzo Mingione and Alberto Martinelli with Fei Xiaotong, 1984

Note by Maurice Bloch[3]**:** The event was the visit of Professor Fei to the LSE Anthropology department, when he presented a paper on small businesses in me-

---

[2] Enzo Mingione is Professor of Sociology at the University of Milano-Bicocca, Italy, and previously Dean of the Faculty of Sociology.

[3] Professor Maurice Bloch is Professor Emeritus of the Department of Anthropology, London School of Economics and Political Science.

dium-sized towns, in fact following up his famous early research. I was then head of the department and chaired the seminar.

H.E. Fei Xiaotong and Professor Maurice Bloch, 1986
Photo sourse: LSE Library's photostream

DOI https://doi.org/10.24103/GCSS1.en.2015.13

List of Contributors[1]

Xiangqun Chang (常向群) is President of Global China Institute, Editor of *Journal of China in Comparative Perspective* (JCCP), and Chief Editor of Global Centry Press; Honorary Professor at University College London, Professorial Research Associate at SOAS, University London, UK, and holder of several professorships and senior fellowships at Peking, Renmin, Fudan and Sun Yat-sen universities in China. Her publications in English and Chinese amount to two million words include *Guanxi or Li shang wanglai?: Reciprocity, Social Support Networks*, and *Social Creativity in a Chinese Village* (2009; 2010).

Dongning Feng (冯东宁) is a Senior Lecturer in Translation Studies at SOAS, University of London. He has taught a range of subjects in China, Japan and Britain. His current research interests focus on critical discourse analysis and translation, translators' autonomy, and literary and screen translation. His publications include works on aesthetics and political communication, politics of translation, and translation as political discourse, Chinese cinema, Chinese cultural and literary studies, and a monograph on literature as political philosophy and communication.

Stephan Feuchtwang (王斯福) is an Emeritus Professor of the Department of Anthropology, London School of Economics and Political Science (LSE), where he established the MSc China in Comparative Perspective Programme in 2006, to date the only one of its kind in the world, and acted as founding director of the China in Comparative Perspective Network (CCPN), LSE. He was President of the British Association for Chinese Studies (BACS). Based on his long term studies on popular religion and politics in mainland China and Taiwan he published work on charisma, place, temples and festivals, and civil society. He has been engaging comparative studies exploring the recognition of catastrophic loss, and civilisations and empires. He is author of *After the Event: The Transmission of Grievous Loss in Germany, China and Taiwan* (2011), and *Popular Religion in China: The Imperial Metaphor* (2001).

Gary G. Hamilton (韩格理) is Henry M. Jackson Professor, Department of Sociology and The Jackson School of International Studies, University of Washington (Seattle), formerly Associate Director of the School. He is the author of *Emergent Economies, Divergent Paths, Economic Organization and International Trade in South Korea and Taiwan* (2006), *Commerce and Capitalism in Chinese Societies*

---

[1] Editor's note: This list excludes those guests who made greetings at the conference except for ZHENG Hangsheng, who was co-author of the General Preface of the 'Understanding China and the World' book series when this collection was first published as *Globalization of Chinese Social Sciences: Commemorating the 105th anniversary of the birth of Fei Xiaotong* (Volume 1) in 2015.

(2006), and *The Market Makers: How Retailers Are Changing the Global Economy* (2011). He is also well known in China for introducing Fei Xiaotong's book *From the Soil – The Foundations of Chinese Society* (1994) to the English-speaking world.

ZHENG Hangsheng (郑杭生) (1936–2014) was the founder of Chinese sociology in the modern period. He was an Honorary President of the Chinese Sociological Association (CSA), Vice-president of Renmin University of China and Director of the Centre for Studies of Sociological Theory and Methods, which became the National Key Research Base for Humanities and Social Sciences of the Ministry of Education. He held longstanding leadership roles at the CSA and other state-run sociological planning and governing organizations. His theoretical contribution to sociology consisted of 'five theories': social operation, social transformation, social mutual-construction, practice-structure theory, and localization of the sociological discipline. His prolific output numbered some 400 articles and nearly 100 books, including monographs, co-authored editions and textbooks.

Stevan Harrell (郝瑞) is Professor of Anthropology, School of Environmental and Forest Sciences, University of Washington. He was Curator of Asian Ethnology at the Burke Museum. Currently he works on international scholarly and educational exchange and to research on human-environment interactions in the US, China, and Taiwan. He is the author of many books, including, *Afterword: China's Tangled Web of Heritage, Cultural Heritage Politics in China* (2013), *Ways of Being Ethnic in Southwest China* (2002), *Mountain Patterns: The Survival of the Nuosu Culture in China* (2000), and *Human Families: Social Change in Global Perspective* (1998).

Harro von Senger (胜雅律) is Professor of Sinology, University of Freiburg and (since 1982) Expert of the Swiss Institute of Comparative Law at Lausanne. He is also an expert on the Chinese military, and author of *The 36 Stratagems for Business: Achieve Your Objectives through Hidden and Unconventional Strategies and Tactics* and *The Book of Stratagems: Tactics for Triumph and Survival*, which has been translated into 14 languages.

Lianyi Song (宋连谊) is Principal Teaching Fellow in Chinese at the Department of the Languages and Cultures of China and Inner Asia, School of Oriental and African Studies (SOAS), University of London. He has taught Chinese as a foreign language in the UK for over 20 years both before and after he obtained his PhD. He is author and co-author of many books, such as *Teach Yourself Beginner's Mandarin Chinese, Get Talking Mandarin Chinese in Ten Days, Speak Mandarin Chinese with Confidence, Beginner's Chinese, Mandarin Chinese Conversation,* and *Read and Write Chinese Script.*

Lik Suen (宣力) is Principal Teaching Fellow in Chinese at the Department of the Languages and Cultures of China and Inner Asia, and Deputy Director of the

London Confucius Institute at the School of Oriental and African Studies (SOAS), University of London. She has taught Chinese as a foreign language in Hong Kong, the USA and the UK for nearly 20 years. She is Chief Examiner in Chinese for a major examining body in the UK, editor of *Get Ahead in Chinese*, and co-author of *Chinese in Steps*.

Jing Xu (徐静) is a UK-based social science researcher, with expertise in policy evaluation. Over the past four years, she has been doing research on the implementation and impact of rural policy in China since 1978. Qualified as an immigration legal adviser by the Office of Immigration Services Commissioner in the UK, she previously worked in the private sector for two years. She also enjoys doing voluntary work. During the past few years, she has spent her free time working with a wide variety of charities and NGOs, including United Nations agencies, an environmental charity, Waterloo TimeBank and Protimos: Lawyers against Poverty.

DOI https://doi.org/10.24103/GCSS1.en.2015.14

About the Editors

Stephan Feuchtwang (王斯福) is Emeritus Professor of Anthropology at the London School of Economics (LSE). He established the first centre for social scientific study on China in the UK (1973) at City University London, and the MSc China in Comparative Perspective Programme (2006) at the LSE, to date the only one of its kind in the world. He was Present of the British Association of China Studies (BACS). He has been engaged in research on popular religion and politics in mainland China and Taiwan since 1966, resulting in a number of publications on charisma, place, temples and festivals, and civil society. He has recently been engaged in a comparative project exploring the theme of the recognition of catastrophic loss, including the loss of archive and recall, which in Chinese cosmology and possibly elsewhere is pre-figured in the category of ghosts. Most recently he has been pursuing a project on the comparison of civilizations and empires. He has published more than ten books and a few dozen articles, including *Popular Religion in China: The Imperial Metaphor* (1991, 2001) and *After the Event: The Transmission of Grievous Loss in Germany, China and Taiwan* (2011).

Xiangqun Chang (常向群) is President of Global China Institute, Editor of *Journal of China in Comparative Perspective* (JCCP), and Chief Editor of Global Century Press; Honorary Professor at University College London, Professorial Research Associate at SOAS, University London, UK, and holder of several professorships and senior fellowships at Peking, Renmin, Fudan and Sun Yat-sen universities in China. To date the only UK-based sociologist trained in both China and the UK, she has been working at universities on social scientific studies of China interdisciplinarily since 1991, when she came to the UK as a Visiting Fellow. In the past two-plus decades Xiangqun has conducted about two dozen research projects and published over two million Chinese characters and English words. Based on a thorough and detailed ethnography of a Chinese village with longitudinal comparisons, she developed a general analytical concept – 'recipropriety' (*lishang-wanglai* 礼尚往来) – a Chinese model of reciprocity, relatedness and social networks (see *Guanxi or Li shang wanglai? Reciprocity, Social Support Networks, & Social Creativity in a Chinese Village*, 2010). This 'recipropriety model' is being tested in many projects with both interdisciplinary and comparative approaches.

ZHOU Daming (周大鸣) is Professor of the School of Anthropology and Sociology, Chang Jiang Scholar Distinguished Professor of Ministry of Education, Director of the Ethnic Group Study Centre, Sun Yat-sen University, Deputy Director of Historical Anthropology Research Center, Ministry of Education Humanities and Social Science Key Research Base at Sun Yat-sen University, and Vice-president of the China Union of Anthropological and Ethnological Sciences (UAES), China. He was co-editor of the US-based *Chinese Sociology Anthropology* (1981–2011). He has published nine books and a few dozen articles. His academic contributions have mainly focused on aspects of migration and urbanization, ethnic groups and regional culture, applied anthropology, and construction of anthropological discipline. He is the initiator of urban anthropology research in China and constructed the theme, method and theoretical basis for the study of urban anthropology in China. He has also used the theory of ethnic group and ethnic group relations to carry out regional cultural studies in China. In the field of applied anthropology, he has undertaken various commissioned projects of the World Bank, the Asian Development Bank, relevant ministries and commissions of the State Council, the Guangdong Provincial Government and other institutions and departments.